THE UPPER ROOM

WHERE THE WORLD MEETS TO PRAY

Susan Hibbins
UK Editor

INTERDENOMINATIONAL
INTERNATIONAL
INTERRACIAL

33 LANGUAGES
Multiple formats are available in some languages

The Bible Reading Fellowship
15 The Chambers, Vineyard
Abingdon OX14 3FE
brf.org.uk

The Bible Reading Fellowship (BRF) is a Registered Charity (233280)

ISBN 978 0 85746 773 7
All rights reserved

Originally published in the USA by The Upper Room®
US edition © The Upper Room®
This edition © The Bible Reading Fellowship 2019
Cover image © Thinkstock

Acknowledgements

Scripture quotations marked NRSV are taken from The New Revised Standard Version of the Bible, Anglicised Edition, copyright © 1989, 1995 by the Division of Christian Education of the National Council of the Churches of Christ in the USA. Used by permission. All rights reserved.

Scripture quotations marked NIV are taken from The Holy Bible, New International Version (Anglicised edition) copyright © 1979, 1984, 2011 by Biblica. Used by permission of Hodder & Stoughton Publishers, an Hachette UK company. All rights reserved. 'NIV' is a registered trademark of Biblica. UK trademark number 1448790.

Extracts marked KJV are from the Authorised Version of the Bible (The King James Bible), the rights in which are vested in the Crown, are reproduced by permission of the Crown's Patentee, Cambridge University Press.

Extracts from CEB copyright © 2011 by Common English Bible.

Printed by Gutenberg Press, Tarxien, Malta

How to use *The Upper Room*

The Upper Room is ideal in helping us spend a quiet time with God each day. Each daily entry is based on a passage of scripture, and is followed by a meditation and prayer. Each person who contributes a meditation to the magazine seeks to relate their experience of God in a way that will help those who use *The Upper Room* every day.

Here are some guidelines to help you make best use of *The Upper Room*:

1   Read the passage of scripture. It is a good idea to read it more than once, in order to have a fuller understanding of what it is about and what you can learn from it.
2   Read the meditation. How does it relate to your own experience? Can you identify with what the writer has outlined from their own experience or understanding?
3   Pray the written prayer. Think about how you can use it to relate to people you know, or situations that need your prayers today.
4   Think about the contributor who has written the meditation. Some users of the *The Upper Room* include this person in their prayers for the day.
5   Meditate on the 'Thought for the day' and the 'Prayer focus', perhaps using them again as the focus for prayer or direction for action.

Why is it important to have a daily quiet time? Many people will agree that it is the best way of keeping in touch every day with the God who sustains us, and who sends us out to do his will and show his love to the people we encounter each day. Meeting with God in this way reassures us of his presence with us, helps us to discern his will for us and makes us part of his worldwide family of Christian people through our prayers.

I hope that you will be encouraged as you use the magazine regularly as part of your daily devotions, and that God will richly bless you as you read his word and seek to learn more about him.

Susan Hibbins
UK Editor

CAN YOU HELP?

Here at BRF, we're always looking for ways to promote the practice of daily Bible reading, and we would like to ask for your help in spreading the word about this valuable resource.

Can I ask you to spread the word about the usefulness of *The Upper Room* in aiding daily meditation and prayer? This could be among your friends and contacts, or at any events in which you might be involved, such as church or a Bible study group, or a conference, special service, retreat or workshop.

We would really value your help, and we'll happily send you some sample copies if you can use them. Just let me know how many you would like and I'll arrange for them to be sent to you. If you wish you can email me at **susan. hibbins@brf.org.uk**.

If you're active on social media, we can supply cover graphics for use on Twitter, Facebook and so on, and we can also supply information packs to churches and groups if you pass on any requests to me.

Thank you in advance for helping us to publicise our Bible reading notes.

Susan Hibbins
UK Editor, The Upper Room

Living as Easter people

This Jesus, God raised up. We are all witnesses to that fact.
Acts 2:32 (CEB)

In the season following Easter, it seems that Jesus' death and resurrection should have utterly transformed the world. Jesus is risen! He has appeared to his disciples, and the Holy Spirit dwells within us. And yet, the world still suffers violence and unrest. People still become ill and face persecution. For Jesus' first followers it might have seemed easier to reflect on the incredible events and life of Jesus Christ with gratitude and awe but then move in a less challenging direction than the one to which Christ called them.

At times, it is tempting to give up, to turn away from a confusing calling or a challenging ministry or the exhausting good work God has called us to. But as many of the writers in this issue remind us, the difficult times often give us the opportunity to experience God's presence anew and reclaim our identities as his beloved children. They remind us that following Christ is not without difficulties, but it is worth it in the end. When we hold on to the promise of new life in Christ and remain persistent in prayer and steadfast in faithful living, we claim the hope of resurrection that the season of Easter embodies.

Living as Easter people amidst the challenges of daily life is not easy, but together – as the body of Christ – we can remind one another of the hope and joy that God offers to us all. As we travel this season together, I pray that the honest words of struggle and encouragement in this issue will give you strength to persevere when life is not easy and that the stories of joy will help you to celebrate the good life made possible through Jesus Christ.

Lindsay L. Gray
Editorial Director, The Upper Room

Hindi
The Council of Communication, Literature, and Publication and the Lucknow Publishing House organised an *Upper Room* writing workshop in Lucknow, India. Thirty-three people submitted meditations for publication as a result!

Odia
The Odia edition team is partnering with Christian youth organisations and local pastors to host small groups for fellowship and to share *The Upper Room* with young people.

Editions of
The Upper Room
are printed in:
- India
  - English
  - Gujarati
  - Hindi
  - Kannada
  - Malayalam
  - Odia
  - Telugu
- Nepal
- Pakistan
- Sri Lanka
  - English
  - Sinhala
  - Tamil

Gifts to the international editions of
The Upper Room help the world meet to pray.

upperroom.org/gift

The Editor writes...

Recently my daily Bible reading was Acts 10:34–43. In it, Peter speaks of God's love for every nation and people, giving an account of Jesus' life, death and resurrection, through which all those who believe in him will receive forgiveness of their sins. In just ten short verses, Peter reveals the purposes of God for the world and for every person in it.

Towards the end of the passage, Peter describes how he and the other disciples were chosen to become Jesus' witnesses, commanded to carry on Jesus' mission and to preach the good news. They are, he says, those 'who ate and drank with him after he rose from the dead' (v. 41, NIV). Apart from illustrating Jesus' human life, I wonder what was on Peter's mind just then.

Did he remember the meal on the beach (John 21:1–13), when Jesus cooked breakfast for his friends? Did he think of the silvery dawn light breaking over the water, and the leap in his heart when he realised that the figure on the shore was Jesus? And, most importantly, did he remember how Jesus talked to him later, forgiving Peter's earlier denial (John 18:15–18) and commissioning him to 'feed my sheep' (John 21:17)? It was the moment that Peter's new life as Jesus' 'rock' really began.

How do we see ourselves, as part of God's eternal plan? Maybe the idea seems too daunting. Who are we to be witnesses for Jesus? To me, these few words that Peter included in his description of good news for the world remind us that our lives as Christians begin simply: in forming a friendship with Jesus. It is us, you and I, who Jesus waits for on the beach; he is happy to sit down with us in that lovely setting and cook us breakfast. He will forgive, commission and send us out in the same way as he sent Peter and all the other disciples, to continue his work, to bring his love and friendship to those we meet and, in so doing, to further God's purposes in the world.

Susan Hibbins
UK Editor

The Bible readings are selected with great care, and we urge you to include the suggested reading in your devotional time.

Visiting Willy

Read John 6:43–48

I have placed before you an open door that no one can shut. I know that you have little strength, yet you have kept my word and have not denied my name.
Revelation 3:8 (NIV)

I remember the sound of the gravel under my tyres as I drove up the lane to visit my friend Willy. I can still see him waving from his porch – one arm extended and the other leaning on his walking stick. 'What took you so long?' he'd ask.

'I stopped to ask some deer for directions.' This joke always made him laugh. We'd sit and talk about nature, his children and how the stroke had made him angry and less motivated. I mostly listened. He just needed to be heard. Willy had a long history of drug abuse, alcoholism, wrong turns and pain that he carried deep inside.

I visited Willy for about a year and watched him grow weaker over time. He wouldn't talk about God. 'That isn't for me. I am okay as I am,' he'd say. One rainy afternoon, as I pulled into Willy's drive, he walked unsteadily towards me through the tall grass to welcome me. 'I did it!' he exclaimed.

'Did what?' I asked.

'You know – went down to the old church and got sorted.' I smiled and shook my head with an awesome feeling of fulfilment. We chuckled and walked back to his garden. In the last months of Willy's life, the Holy Spirit had called him to walk through the church doors and forever be with God.

Prayer: *Heavenly Father, thank you for opportunities to share your love and grace with others. Amen*

Thought for the day: My small actions can make a huge difference in someone's life of faith.

Matt Simmons (Kentucky, US)

I can do it

Read Exodus 4:1–12

[The Lord] said to me, 'My grace is sufficient for you, for my power is made perfect in weakness.' Therefore I will boast all the more gladly about my weaknesses, so that Christ's power may rest on me.
2 Corinthians 12:9 (NIV)

Although I had joined a Christian church group almost two years earlier, I had never taken a prominent role in its ministry. One day I got a message from our leader that said, 'Meli, you have had a lot of extraordinary experiences, so I want you to give the sermon the last week of this month.' Feeling inadequate, I refused and told him that I had a fear of public speaking. The leader replied that I needed to start speaking in front of people so I could become more comfortable with it.

Then I remembered that when God first called Moses to lead the Israelites out of Egypt, Moses refused several times, saying that he was not an eloquent speaker (Exodus 4:10). But in spite of Moses' weaknesses, God still used him to lead a great nation, Israel, out of Egypt towards the promised land.

We all have weaknesses, but we don't have to let those become an excuse to refuse the work God calls us to do. God doesn't rely on our weaknesses but on our willingness to rely on his strength. This can give us full confidence to aim our best efforts towards doing great things to his glory.

Prayer: *Dear God, we have many weaknesses, but we know that we can do anything because you are our strength. Amen*

Thought for the day: 'I can do all things through [Christ] who strengthens me' (Philippians 4:13, NRSV).

Meliana Santoso (East Java, Indonesia)

Steadfast love

Read Romans 8:35–39

Give thanks to the God of heaven. His love endures forever.
Psalm 136:26 (NIV)

Several years ago I took on a devotional challenge in which participants choose a word to concentrate on for the year. I chose the word 'love', initially focusing on examining my love for God. To reinforce my commitment, I pinned up a photo in my office of a heart drawn in the sand on the beach with waves crashing nearby. Inside the heart was another heart saying, 'Love God'. One morning a colleague noticed the image and said, 'Wouldn't it be great if after the waves crash over it, the words "Love God" were still there?' He smiled and walked away, saying, 'Not likely, is it?'

His remark made me reflect again on what it means to love God. Just how steadfast is my love for God? Is my love for him 'written in the sand' only in good times? When things get tough, is my love for God still readily spoken, tangible, visible? How likely am I to declare firmly that I love God after a storm has come and the waves of loss, grief, disappointment, rejection and fear have crashed over me?

The questions I asked myself still remain. But after reading Psalm 136, I was thankful, knowing that God's love for me will always stand.

Prayer: *O God, help us to remember that your love for us is infinite and everlasting. May we remain steadfast in our love for you in every situation. Amen*

Thought for the day: God's love is steadfast. Is mine?

Cassius Rhue (South Carolina, US)

Facing change

Read Isaiah 33:2–6

[The Lord] will be the sure foundation for your times, a rich store of salvation and wisdom and knowledge; the fear of the Lord is the key to this treasure.

Isaiah 33:6 (NIV)

The day was hot, but inside my heart felt cold and fragile. Tears streaked down my face as my twin boys headed off to college. My day-to-day mothering came to a screeching halt that morning, leaving me to face an empty nest.

Later that week, a pair of doves built a nest on my trellis. When their babies hatched, the nest hummed with activity. The parents worked constantly to feed the hungry chicks. The babies grew quickly, and soon the nest became too crowded. One morning, I noticed that the nest was empty. The doves – not just the chicks, but the parents as well – had moved on.

The birds taught me that God designed our lives to have changing roles and seasons. As I watched the birds, God prompted me to seek a new role for my new season – in this case, a second career as a writer.

As we face the changing seasons of our lives, we can go to God for stability, wisdom and knowledge. Thankfully, God weaves blessings into each season of life.

Prayer: *Dear Lord, help us to face each change with faith. We ask that you would provide stability, wisdom and strength so that we may adapt to new roles and seasons well. Amen*

Thought for the day: God will help me adapt to each new season of life.

May Patterson (Alabama, US)

Like a child

Read Mark 10:46–52

Whoever becomes humble like this child is the greatest in the kingdom of heaven.
Matthew 18:4 (NRSV)

A minister friend of mine was recruiting volunteers to portray biblical characters at a special church service. Knowing that I enjoyed acting, she asked me to play Bartimaeus, the blind beggar who called out to get Jesus' attention. As the children rotated through several Bible scenes in groups of four or five, I sat cross-legged, with my eyes closed tight, calling out, 'Jesus, have mercy on me!' With each group, the teacher read the story from the Bible, and then the group moved on to the next scene. To my surprise, after one group moved on, one child turned back. I was about to open my eyes when I heard her footsteps and felt her small hands on my head. 'Jesus loves you,' she said, 'and he has given you back your sight!'

I was deeply touched that this child had not been content to leave the blind beggar alone, still wanting to meet Jesus. I wondered how often I have avoided reaching out to a hurting person. When could I have shared words of hope with someone in need? This child's faith has inspired me to take the time to talk with others about Jesus' love.

Prayer: *God of love and mercy, help us to have the faith of children, and may we live out that faith in how we interact with others. Amen*

Thought for the day: I will trust Jesus with a childlike faith as I reach out to those in need.

Jim Harris (Virginia, US)

Learning from bees

Read 1 Corinthians 12:4–14
The body is not made up of one part but of many.
1 Corinthians 12:14 (NIV)

In February 2017 the government moved my family, neighbours and friends in the La Barquita community in Santo Domingo, in the Dominican Republic. We were all relocated to a new community with better living conditions. A week after I moved into my new house, however, a swarm of bees arrived. I was unsure what to do; I did not want to harm them, but I also did not want to share my home with them.

I hoped that through prayer I would be able to determine what God was trying to teach me through the bees, so I asked my church family to pray with me. I then turned to the Bible. When I read 1 Corinthians 12:12–13, I recalled that bee colonies are united in their work to produce honey and to keep their colony healthy.

We can follow the example of unity we see in bee colonies by working towards God's purpose in harmony as a family, congregation and community. When we come together for the greater goal of furthering God's kingdom, we can be as unified and effective as a bee colony, working as one body.

Prayer: *Almighty God, help us to work for your kingdom, united through Christ. Amen*

Thought for the day: I am one of many members of the body of Christ.

Andrea Ramírez Zabala (Puerto Rico)

Finding the food

Read Matthew 28:16–20

Jesus replied, 'It's written, People won't live only by bread, but by every word spoken by God.'
Matthew 4:4 (CEB)

When I was a young boy in the 1950s, my family would visit my mother's parents in Ohio. Their house backed on to a busy railway line. The rear entrance to their house had a porch – and more often than not after playing with my cousins I would find a homeless man sitting on the porch eating a sandwich with a glass of milk that our grandmother had prepared for him.

I asked Grandpa why the men always came to their house instead of any of the others in the row by the railway line. He took me down to the railway and showed me how some of the sleepers directly behind his house had paint or chalk markings on them. He said, 'This is how the homeless people tell one another where to find food.' They used whatever they could find to mark the sleepers.

That lesson from my grandfather is one reason I participate in prison ministry – to help others find food for their souls. As Christ-followers we are to tell others where to find the real nourishment for life: God's word. Jesus didn't tell us to go build churches and invite our friends and neighbours. He told us to go and tell others where to 'find the food'!

Prayer: *Dear God, guide us in our efforts to show and tell others your life-giving word. Amen*

Thought for the day: God wants us to show others how to find the food of life.

Martyn Haynes (California, US)

A talent to share

Read Exodus 23:6–9

Don't take advantage of poor or needy workers, whether they are fellow Israelites or immigrants who live in your land.
Deuteronomy 24:14 (CEB)

As a volunteer with new refugees coming into my town, it breaks my heart when I hear so many stories of unscrupulous people taking advantage of them. I wonder how I can help them, even when my energy and time are limited. I met Aung Lin and his daughters last autumn and then visited him over Christmas. He had stepped on a land mine in a refugee camp in Thailand, losing one foot, both hands and his eyesight. Then his wife died. When he came to Nebraska with his four daughters, a couple from his ethnic group in Burma agreed to take them into their home. I hoped that in some small way I could help this family. When I visit Aung Lin, I hope that along with the rice, fruit and money I bring, I also brighten his day by showing God's love to him.

God has given talents and skills to each of us for helping others. Those who love to sew help refugees to learn these skills. A craft group has been organised to help earn money for the refugee families. A retired teacher helps the new students with their homework. My 81-year-old friend Sunny helps the refugees to learn about the customs and culture of our area. Whether with a refugee, a lonely elderly person or someone at church who is ill – each of us has a talent that can be shared to the glory of God.

Prayer: *Dear God, open our minds and hearts to ways that we can be of help and encouragement to others. Amen*

Thought for the day: Every day I can depend on God to show me someone in need.

Nancy R. Meyer (Nebraska, US)

Joyful prayer

Read Luke 11:5–13

Do not be anxious about anything, but in every situation, by prayer and petition, with thanksgiving, present your requests to God.
Philippians 4:6 (NIV)

When I returned home from the market with my groceries, my three-year-old son, Alan, spotted the biscuits I had bought. He exclaimed loudly, 'Papa, biscuits!' Then suddenly he began to cry as he kept asking for them. Alan's behaviour made me a little sad. I thought, 'Why doesn't he ask with a smile? Doesn't he trust me?'

I began to think about the way I ask something of God. Often, like Alan, instead of asking God trustingly, I burst into tears and keep crying for the same thing again and again. God is pleased to hear our requests, but the apostle Paul says we are not to be anxious as we pray. I know that I sometimes forget Jesus' promise: 'Ask and it will be given to you; seek and you will find; knock and the door will be opened to you' (Matthew 7:7).

God knows what we need before we even ask, but he wants us to ask with faith and thanksgiving. He wants to fill our lives with love and joy, and he will do so. That's why God sent Jesus – to bring us abundant life (see John 10:10).

Prayer: *Loving God, give us hearts full of faith so that we may receive in abundance. Amen*

Thought for the day: I will approach God today with trust and thanksgiving.

Hiteshkumar Jashvantbhai Solanki (Gujarat, India)

Hope out of despair

Read Zephaniah 3:14–20

The Lord, your God, is in your midst… He will rejoice over you with gladness, he will renew you in his love; he will exult over you with loud singing.
Zephaniah 3:17 (NRSV)

In my first term at college, I found myself floundering, depressed and unsure of myself. No major event had triggered these feelings; I couldn't explain why I felt so alone. While I still believed in God, I began to doubt that my life was worth anything to him. It was a struggle just to get out of bed every morning and go through the motions of each day.

Though that year was painful, I did learn one crucial lesson: that God is never nearer to me than when I am suffering. And that suffering was not a punishment from God; rather, it forced me to stop relying on my own strength and abilities. I learned to lean on God and the powerful truths of the Bible, not on my own unpredictable emotions. God loves me. He has good plans for my life. He does not hold my sins against me. Those truths anchored my soul amid the storm-tossed waves.

As I navigated my depression, my prayer life grew and deepened. My heart clung to the truths in the Bible. Gradually, through the help of many who reached out to me, prayed with me, encouraged me and counselled me, I found my way out of despair. Then I realised that I had not been abandoned; instead, God had filled me with hope.

Prayer: *Dear God, when we're tempted to despair, teach us to put our hope in you. Amen*

Thought for the day: When I'm hurting, God is near.

Kate Underwood (Illinois, US)

Transformed

Read Romans 12:1–3

Do not be conformed to this world, but be transformed by the renewing of your minds, so that you may discern what is the will of God – what is good and acceptable and perfect.
Romans 12:2 (NRSV)

I was approaching my older years when God let me know in no uncertain terms that my many years of prodigal-son-type bad behaviour – excessive drinking and gambling, for instance – needed to come to an end. After crashing my truck into a tree during one of my drunken stupors, I finally saw a clear choice: I could allow God to rule the rest of my life, or I could choose the world. I made the decision to let God's love, grace and forgiveness convert me into a fruitful Christian, beginning with repentance and breaking away from the wasteful life I had led for 55 years.

Abstaining from that lifestyle of reckless behaviour changed my life to one worth living – fasting from my worldly ways in order to feast on God's word. I now try to serve others and give back in gratitude for all God has given me. I will always be a Christian who is under construction, attempting to refrain from the bad habits that plagued me for so many years. But now I have a Saviour who has transformed me into a wiser, loving and more caring person.

Prayer: *Dear God, guide us each day so that we may come to love you more and do your will. In Jesus' name, we pray. Amen*

Thought for the day: I will serve God by serving others.

John Groves (Maryland, US)

A mother's faith

Read Matthew 7:13–14

[Jesus said,] 'Make every effort to enter through the narrow door, because many, I tell you, will try to enter and will not be able to.'
Luke 13:24 (NIV)

A devout follower of Jesus Christ, my mum has emailed a 'Weekly Inspiration' to her children, friends and colleagues for over five years. Each of these emails contains an inspiring and motivational message that has served as a guide for me on how to live out the week ahead through believing and having faith in God. My mum's relationship with God always serves as an example for me of what Jesus meant when he said, 'Make every effort to enter through the narrow door.'

Mum has always made her best effort in her own journey towards salvation, and is constantly finding new ways to spread the word of Christ and lead others to him. From her weekly inspirations, to distributing *The Upper Room*, to being an active church member, my mum inspires me to be a better person and to make sure I am putting forth my best effort so that I may be able to enter into God's kingdom.

Prayer: *Dear God, each day give us the courage and strength to live out our lives according to your will. Amen*

Thought for the day: Today I will find new ways to inspire others to share the good news of Christ.

Clint Bowman (North Carolina, US)

Before we even speak

Read Luke 7:11–17

'Before they call I will answer.'
Isaiah 65:24 (NIV)

One day while driving to work, I was troubled about a task that God had asked me to do. I was late for work, caught in traffic, so I decided to listen to the radio. During the programme someone gave a testimony that provided strength and clarity for my own struggle. I knew then that I had experienced God's promise: even before we pray the Lord will answer.

This reminded me of the story of the funeral of a widow's son in a town called Nain, as recorded in Luke's gospel. As the procession was leaving the town gates, it met with Jesus. Before the widow even opened her mouth, Jesus raised her son from death. Jesus saw her heart – and in love and great empathy gave the son back to his mother alive!

God is truly our ever-present help in times of need. When we are living with sorrow or confusion, we can remember that he sees our hearts and will answer us – often before we even speak.

Prayer: *Dear Lord, help us in the midst of pain and confusion not to forget your presence. May we at all times be sensitive to your voice. In Jesus' name. Amen*

Thought for the day: God knows my pain even before I give voice to it.

Neliswa Shauna Chigudu (Johannesburg, South Africa)

Encouragement

Read Acts 15:30–35

Judas and Silas, who themselves were prophets, said much to encourage and strengthen the believers.
Acts 15:32 (NIV)

Life was difficult for new Christians in the first century because the culture they lived in was not attuned to the ways of Christ. When people persecuted them for their beliefs, they became discouraged. Judas and Silas are two whom God sent to encourage other believers, to help their faith become stronger. In fact the words 'encourage' and 'encouragement' are used countless times in the New Testament. Throughout the centuries, receiving encouragement has been important to all Christians as they grow and mature in their faith.

One morning when I was attending a conference and praying about something special I could do that day, God nudged me to focus on encouraging others. That day God sent several people my way who needed encouragement. As far as I could tell, I did not make a huge difference in anyone's life. It could be that someone's life was changed and I didn't know about it. But that day I did learn that people appreciate and are strengthened by words of encouragement. I also learned that each of us is encouraged even as we encourage others.

Prayer: *Dear God, lead us to people who need encouragement and give us the words to strengthen their faith. Amen*

Thought for the day: God can use me to encourage others.

Tom Kennedy (Texas, US)

Not afraid

Read Psalm 112:6–8
[The righteous] will have no fear of bad news; their hearts are steadfast, trusting in the Lord.
Psalm 112:7 (NIV)

Recently, my doctor told me that I have a rare tumour called dermatofibrosarcoma. When I heard the news, two choices came to my mind: I could succumb to fear, or I could have faith in Jesus, my Lord. When I found the wonderful verse above, it helped me not to panic or worry about the bad news that I heard from my doctor.

The Lord assured me that I did not need to fear bad news. Like the righteous ones in Psalm 112, I could stand steadfast and be encouraged, confidently relying on the Lord. Yes, the news is bad. My family depends on me to take care of their daily needs, and I do worry about them. But I trust in the Lord, who promised to be a great help in times of trouble and always to be present with us (see Psalm 46).

We all face difficulties, but trusting the Lord can relieve us of the weight of worry. It is easy to let fear control our minds when we hear bad news, but fear will not control us when we put our trust in the Lord.

Prayer: *Dear Lord, in times of trouble give us the courage to face each day knowing that you are greater than all our worry and fear. Amen*

Thought for the day: The Lord's faithfulness is greater than my problems.

Ismelalem Woldegiorgis (British Columbia, Canada)

A way through

Read Isaiah 43:1–7

No testing has overtaken you that is not common to everyone. God is faithful, and he will not let you be tested beyond your strength, but… will also provide the way out so that you may be able to endure it.
1 Corinthians 10:13 (NRSV)

Many people who are trying to comfort someone experiencing tragedy say, 'God never gives us more than we can handle.' But this can backfire, making the sufferer feel worse. They may say, 'If God is sending me these crises because I'm so strong, then I don't want to be strong.'

This modern saying is a paraphrase of part of 1 Corinthians 10:13, but the full verse actually says something quite different and far deeper. The full verse points out that life – not God – sends adversity to us all. Our trials are a common experience, and knowing this is in itself reassuring. Empathy and shared struggles can work miracles. The text also points out that sometimes we are tested beyond our resources and strength. Sometimes we are overwhelmed by life's trials, and sometimes it is more than we can handle.

But understanding this, God gives us something to enable us to endure. The apostle Paul assures us that when we are tested beyond our strength, God will provide a way through until, free on the other side, we can walk forward into the light of a new day.

Prayer: *Dear God, give us eyes to see the way through that you offer us in times of adversity and the faith to trust your promise before it comes. Amen*

Thought for the day: When life is too hard, God will provide a way through.

Hope Harle-Mould (New York, US)

God's love song

Read Romans 8:14–21

How beautiful your sandalled feet, O prince's daughter!
Song of Songs 7:1 (NIV)

When my husband and I were living in Nicaragua as missionaries, I struggled with the relentless heat. Getting through the day and doing a few basic chores were often all I could manage. I suffered from migraines and frequently wondered what I was doing there. I wasn't sure I would ever acclimatise enough to be able to do anything useful.

I wrote today's quoted scripture in my journal after arriving in Nicaragua. It came to mind one morning as I sat looking at my feet. 'How beautiful your sandalled feet, O prince's daughter!' Reading this verse, I was overwhelmed when I remembered that I am the daughter of the King: precious, loved, cherished and honoured. I know God's delight in me and love for me. Whenever I doubted what I was doing in Nicaragua; I could look at my sandalled feet and remember who I am. It didn't matter if I was able to accomplish great things while in Nicaragua; I was precious to God no matter what.

We are beautiful, not because of what we do or achieve but because we belong to God. May this knowledge comfort and encourage us, reminding us of our purpose regardless of what we accomplish.

Prayer: *Loving God, help us to walk through today in the certainty of your love for us. Help us to remember our purpose in you. Amen*

Thought for the day: I don't have to earn God's love.

Jodie Dennis (Northamptonshire, United Kingdom)

Our patient God

Read Isaiah 40:27–31

Those who wait for the Lord shall renew their strength.
Isaiah 40:31 (NRSV)

When I was about five years old I had a heart condition called endocarditis. In those days this disease was very serious, and my life was threatened for almost a year. My family members were not Christians; but because we lived in a small town, the Sunday school in the local church heard about me and sent a teacher and a small group of children called 'The Sunshine Club' to visit me.

I don't remember much about the visit, but I recall that they gave me a small shiny picture of Jesus holding a lamb. It said underneath that Jesus is the good shepherd. The children wrote some kind messages on the back of it, in pencil. Somehow, through all our family's moves and the many moves my wife and I made during our marriage, I managed to keep that little picture. The pencil inscriptions have faded but are still readable.

Later in my Christian life, the picture became one of my prized possessions. It reminded me that God is faithful and patient with us, waiting and being available when we finally realise our need for him. As the verse above says, 'Those who wait for the Lord shall renew their strength.' I gained spiritual strength and physical healing, and I am still going strong at 85 years old. God is faithful and true, and the sooner we come to him, the longer we can honour him and walk with Jesus Christ.

Prayer: *Dear Lord, bless all who have been touched by your care, and bring them to a true faith in Jesus our Saviour. Amen*

Thought for the day: I will follow as God leads me to help others start their journey to faith.

Ken Claar (Idaho, US)

Learning to forgive

Read Matthew 5:43–48

Jesus said, 'Father, forgive them, for they do not know what they are doing.'
Luke 23:34 (NIV)

Many years ago when I was seven and my brother was three, I witnessed a group of adults bullying my mother because she was of Japanese heritage. Even though I was too young to understand why this happened, I was angry and felt hatred. I knew that if my dad had been at home, instead of serving in the army overseas, these people would not have dared to do what they did. I saw my mother cry many times while my dad was away. It was difficult for me to understand why we, as a family, all had to suffer.

It took some time for me to understand that as Christians, we are called to forgive those who hurt us or our loved ones. I think one of the hardest things God asks us to do is to 'love your enemies and pray for those who persecute you' (Matthew 5:44), as Jesus did on the cross. Though I have never forgotten, I have forgiven those people for the evil they did. For me, it is like a painful wound that has healed, but the scar remains as a constant reminder of what happened. The words of Jesus and his example have taught me a great deal about forgiveness.

Prayer: *Dear Father, thank you for forgiving our sins as we forgive those who sin against us. Amen*

Thought for the day: When I forgive, God heals me.

Eileen Thrift (Florida, US)

God will make a way

Read Luke 12:22–34

You will keep in perfect peace those whose minds are steadfast, because they trust in you.
Isaiah 26:3 (NIV)

I am a banker and a part-time minister. Recently, I was faced with the possibility of dismissal from my job. My first reaction was fear and concern for my wife and our young son. I was also upset because I felt as though my possible dismissal meant that my work for the past four years at the organisation had not been sufficient. I tried to act as if all were well when I was at work, but I was deeply troubled by my situation.

Before I went to sleep one night, I took my concerns to the Lord in prayer. When I woke up the following morning, a word from the Lord came to remind me of God's ability to clothe the wild flowers of the fields and to feed the birds of the air so they never have to worry (Luke 12:22–34). This reminder of God's blessings relieved the heaviness in my heart and reminded me of the possibilities and provisions of the Lord. This insight continues to sustain my belief that God will provide for my needs even if I lose my job.

When we are faced with scary possibilities, it can be easy to worry and feel as if we are alone. During times of worry and uncertainty, we can cast our cares on God. The Lord opens pathways for us when we don't see a way on our own.

Prayer: *Dear Lord, thank you for making a way for us. Help us remember to trust you when we begin to worry or fear for our future. Amen*

Thought for the day: Each new day brings reassurance from God.

Hassan A. Bello (Kaduna, Nigeria)

The pattern

Read Exodus 31:1–11

Choose life, so that you and your children may live and that you may love the Lord your God, listen to his voice, and hold fast to him.
Deuteronomy 30:19–20 (NIV)

I enjoy dressmaking, knitting and other similar crafts, but in order to make something I have to have a pattern. It's no good my taking a length of material, scissors, and needle and thread; the finished item would never fit properly. But given a pattern and instructions I can produce an attractive, well-fitting garment.

Today's reading is about Bezalel and Oholiab, two men who were both skilled craftsmen, but they too had to work according to a pattern. The instructions for their work were given to Moses and they had to follow them to produce acceptable products.

It occurred to me that our lives are the same: if we live according to our own ideas we are almost certain to end up in a mess. In the Bible, however, we are given a pattern for life – lived according to God's plan and instruction for us. As the above verse reiterates, in doing so we are choosing life, listening to God's voice and holding fast to him.

Prayer: *Dear Lord, help us always to live our lives according to the pattern you have given us. Amen*

Thought for the day: The pattern is there for me to follow.

Hilary Hartley (Sussex, England)

Keep watch

Read Matthew 26:31–46

[Jesus] said to them, 'My soul is overwhelmed with sorrow to the point of death. Stay here and keep watch with me.'
Matthew 26:38 (NIV)

As Jesus approached the moment of his betrayal, he was fully aware of the dreadful task ahead. He wanted to draw near to God and took his closest disciples with him. When Jesus wanted to approach his Father in prayer, he told his disciples to wait and keep watch with him. Although they could not do anything about his sorrow or the task ahead, he needed their companionship.

Jesus' request of his disciples reminds me of when I was younger and playing school sports. We were taught that even if we weren't playing, we should always be excited and engaged in the game. We were told to cheer for our teammates, pay attention to what was going on and stay ready just in case we were called on to play.

Unfortunately, when we are not on the frontlines, sometimes we disengage; we stop being available and fall asleep on the work of God altogether. God wants us to be engaged and ready for ministry. A part of communing with him is supporting the faithful work of others and staying alert for the time when he will call us into action.

Prayer: *Dear Lord, even when we don't seem to have an active part, help us remain engaged with and excited for the work you are doing. Amen*

Thought for the day: When God calls, I will be ready.

Gordon Rowe (Indiana, US)

Refuge from the storm

Read Psalm 46:1–11

The Lord is my rock, my fortress and my deliverer; my God is my rock, in whom I take refuge, my shield and the horn of my salvation, my stronghold.
Psalm 18:2 (NIV)

When Hurricane María hit Puerto Rico, my husband and I were terrified. We felt helpless when faced with the fury of the hurricane assaulting our lovely island. We spent those frightening moments deep in prayer, asking God to be our refuge during the storm.

I was exhausted and felt as if I didn't have the energy to carry on. While feeling intense anxiety, I remembered the psalmist's words: 'God is our refuge and strength, an ever-present help in trouble' (Psalm 46:1). I held fast to God's promise and was able to experience his presence.

During that storm, I learned not to depend on my own strength but to trust in God. I experienced unconditional love while his presence sustained me during that dark, terrifying night, and I have continued to trust in his divine protection. Even during powerful storms, may we all remember that the almighty God is our refuge.

Prayer: *Guardian of our lives, thank you for your constant care and concern for us when we face adversity. Be our refuge when we are weak, and support us with your strength. Amen*

Thought for the day: God is my refuge.

Nereida Reyes Santos (Puerto Rico)

A job we can do

Read Luke 8:32–39

[Jesus said,] 'Return home and tell how much God has done for you.'
So the man went away and told all over the town how much Jesus
had done for him.
Luke 8:39 (NIV)

I used to be afraid that I couldn't do what God expected of me. I had read about the work of the saints since the time of Jesus and knew that I couldn't live up to their accomplishments. So I decided to take a closer look at Jesus' expectations of the people he encountered.

When Jesus healed people, he gave them a variety of instructions. To the paralysed man whose friends had lowered him down through the roof, he said, 'Get up, take your mat and go home' (Luke 5:24). He told a man who had been possessed to 'return home and tell how much God has done for you'. Jesus told the ten lepers, 'Go, show your-selves to the priests' (Luke 17:14). Jesus told his disciples to take up a cross and follow him and to 'go and make disciples of all nations' (Matthew 28:19).

At some point I realised that while Jesus calls all of us to take up our cross and follow him and to make disciples, we are not all called to do that in the same way. Perhaps I can start by simply helping and encour-aging other people whenever the opportunity arises. Our call to serve God will not look like someone else's call. We can be glad that we can serve people in their times of need. God will help each of us to do the job that we are called to do.

Prayer: *Dear Father, bless those who are serving you this day. In Jesus' name. Amen*

Thought for the day: God loves us all and calls us to different tasks.

Thad H. Carter (Texas, US)

Perfect trust

Read Psalm 34:1–8

This poor soul cried, and was heard by the Lord, and was saved from every trouble.
Psalm 34:6 (NRSV)

My five-year-old daughter was eager to help me bake a fruitcake, fetching the flour and the sultanas from the pantry as I read out the ingredients in turn. 'Eggs,' I said, and she opened the fridge. I briefly turned away to retrieve the egg beater from the drawer and – *crash!* – the whole box of eggs splattered on the kitchen floor. I couldn't hide my dismay. Money was short for us, and now we had no eggs. My daughter looked up at me unperturbed. 'Don't worry, Mummy,' she said. 'Daddy can mend them.'

My little girl's faith in her beloved father was the perfect reminder to me of the faith we can have in our heavenly Father's ability to repair the damage in our lives. While my daughter's father could not put broken eggs back together, nothing is impossible for our heavenly Father, who cares for us and waits only to be asked for help. Even if we think our lives are broken beyond repair, our Father can mend them when we entrust our struggles to him.

Prayer: *Loving Father, we bring to you what is broken in our lives. We place the pieces in your loving hands as we ask for and accept your help. Amen*

Thought for the day: When I can't see a way forward, God can.

Dorothy O'Neill (South Australia, Australia)

Extravagant love

Read John 13:1–17

[Jesus said,] 'Now that I, your Lord and Teacher, have washed your feet, you also should wash one another's feet.'
John 13:14 (NIV)

For my birthday my sister gave me a very expensive gift. It was not unusual for her to show such generosity. Ever since she became a believer and servant of Jesus Christ when she was young, my life and the lives of many others have been changed forever by her extravagant love. She shares all she has: food from her bountiful garden, medical knowledge and life wisdom, baking and hours of service. Many people in our community remember her for her years of service as a youth leader, and many more have shared in a community meal served each month at our church.

The radical, humble and extravagant love Jesus showed to his disciples as he washed their feet was hard for them to accept; but that act taught us that we are to serve God by loving and humbly serving others. James 1:22 reminds us, 'Do not merely listen to the word, and so deceive yourselves. Do what it says.' When we accept the love of Jesus, we become vessels that show love to others.

Prayer: *God of love, thank you for the love you poured out on us through your Son. Fill us to overflowing so that we may share your love with others. Amen*

Thought for the day: Today I will look for opportunities to show Christ's love.

Kay Hawk (Ohio, US)

Loving our neighbours

Read Matthew 2:7–12

*No one has greater love than this, to lay down one's life for
one's friends.*
John 15:13 (NRSV)

While serving in Iraq in 2007, I awoke early one morning with an over-whelming sense of dread. I prayed desperately that God would protect me and shield my family from the pain they would experience if I didn't return home. I wrote a letter to my wife and children and asked my officer to ensure that they received it if something happened to me.

Despite my stomach-churning fear, we set out on our mission. On the outskirts of Baghdad, we were halted by the frantic Muslim chief of police with whom I had been working for over a year. He insisted we go no further because the road ahead was full of roadside bombs. After further investigation we found that we had been set up for an attack, and our deaths had been averted by this unexpected messenger.

I still struggle with thoughts of that day, but I take comfort in the friendship that God placed in my path through that devoted and honest man. It would have been easy for him to let us drive past or for me to ignore his warning. My unlikely friend taught me a lesson about love and kindness that day. Our neighbours are often very different from us, but God calls us to seek friendship, kindness and understanding even from those who appear different. Loving all our neighbours opens us up to great blessings.

Prayer: *Heavenly Father, teach us to show kindness to strangers. Help us to treat others the way we want to be treated and to embrace all people as your children. Amen*

Thought for the day: God calls me to show kindness to everyone I meet.

Chad B. McRee (Texas, US)

Opportunity from God

Read Galatians 6:1–10

Let each of you look not to your own interests, but to the interests of others.
Philippians 2:4 (NRSV)

My grandma died when I was a teenager in high school. Before Grandma died, she was unable to walk and often called me to ask for help. At the time, I grumbled at her requests for my help. I thought, 'Why does Grandma always call me, not my brother or sister?' Soon after, Grandma died – and I wept.

When Grandma was alive, my aunt helped to care for her, since my aunt is unmarried and lives with my family. Recently, my aunt was also unable to walk. Unlike Grandma, my aunt rarely called for my help. But her condition reminded me of how I had reacted to Grandma. I wondered, 'Is God giving me a second chance to be selfless and care for my family?'

In Galatians 6, Paul encourages the Galatians to carry each other's burdens. This passage reminds me of the importance of helping others with their physical needs as well as their spiritual needs. Helping others is not an obligation but an opportunity from God. Knowing this, when God asks us to do something for another, we can complete the task with joy.

Prayer: *Dear Lord, help us to use the opportunities you provide to care for others. Guide us to help others in the ways they need us most. Amen*

Thought for the day: I can bless others by responding joyfully when God calls me to help.

Linawati Santoso (East Java, Indonesia)

Be still

Read Exodus 14:10–18
The Lord will fight for you, and you have only to keep still.
Exodus 14:14 (NRSV)

My friend went white-water rafting with a small group, and after going over a class IV rapid, she was thrown out of the raft and into a turbulent part of the river called a weir. Her natural instinct was to fight against the current and try to swim to the top, but she had been coached by her rafting instructor beforehand that the way to survive a fall into a weir is to be still. In this very tense moment, she remembered her instructor's words; she remained still, and the current pushed her out.

What a reminder of Moses' words to the Israelites after God had led them safely to the other side of the Red Sea! 'The Lord will fight for you, and you have only to keep still.' Sometimes, when I'm experiencing turbulent waters in my own life, I find being still to be one of the most difficult things in the world. When Pharaoh's army was within sight and the Israelites felt that their lives were about to end, Moses' word to them was, 'Be still.' When we're confronted with life's challenges, our impulse is often to fight back or maybe to give up. But being still shows our trust that God is greater than our challenges and that even when we are uncertain, he is faithful to us.

Prayer: *Dear God, in times of trial and doubt when we feel helpless, teach us to trust you. Amen*

Thought for the day: Because I trust God, I can remain calm in the midst of crisis.

Adam Benson (North Carolina, US)

Fledgling Christians

Read 1 Peter 2:1–6

Like newborn babies, crave pure spiritual milk, so that by it you may grow up in your salvation.
1 Peter 2:2 (NIV)

Over a period of time, I watched a pair of robins build a nest, hatch their eggs and feed their young. What a busy pair! Once the babies arrived, the parents hopped around the lawn, gathering worms to drop into hungry beaks. Without constant nurturing, those little fluff-balls would not have survived.

As Christians, we can take a few lessons from those birds about nurturing new believers. Just as the birds provided a safe nest, congregations provide a safe place for new believers to ask questions and express doubts. Through worship, sermons and Bible studies, we feed new believers what they need to understand and practise their faith. Through one-to-one conversations and friendships, mature Christians are role models who show new believers how to live out their faith. And just as the parent robins worked as a team, so members of a congregation show teamwork as they exercise their spiritual gifts – giving, teaching and encouraging.

New believers need the church, and the church needs new believers to carry on its mission. What a privilege and joy to hold new believers close to our hearts, to feed them God's word and to protect them until they're ready to fly on their own. Someday, they in turn will nurture other new believers.

Prayer: *Dear Lord, open our eyes to the needs of those new in the faith. Amen*

Thought for the day: Whose faith will I nurture today?

Shirley G. Brosius (Pennsylvania, US)

Wings of a dove

Read 1 Timothy 6:17–19
I wish I had wings like a dove! I'd fly away and rest.
Psalm 55:6 (CEB)

At the college where I teach, one day I gave a special assignment to the first-year students. I asked them to write a prose-poem on the topic, 'If I were given two wings'. Some students started writing straight away, while others hesitated. With some persuasion on my part they all finished within the allotted time, and they presented their poems to the class with a sense of achievement. Among all the good pieces, Salmaan's stood apart. It read, 'Oh, were I blessed with two wings! With them I would fly afar to become wings of those who have no wings.'

Those lines still linger in my mind. With this noble vision Salmaan now teaches at a primary school in Kerala. God gives him opportunities every day to become wings of love and knowledge to many children.

God calls us to surrender ourselves completely, reaching out to others and becoming a source of love, knowledge and healing. The psalmist sought to fly above life-threatening situations to find solace in God's presence, and God empowers us to reach others and to become a source of love and compassion.

Prayer: *Heavenly Father, empower us to become wings of love so that we may reach out to those who are in need. Amen*

Thought for the day: Our divine calling is to be a blessing for others.

Shaji George (Kerala, India)

Being angels

Read 1 Kings 19:3–8

All at once an angel touched him and said, 'Get up and eat.' He looked around, and there by his head was some bread baked over hot coals, and a jar of water.

1 Kings 19:5–6 (NIV)

I was in a trauma ward following a serious car accident. It was the middle of the night and I was hot, in terrible pain and couldn't sleep. A nurse appeared and I asked for water. She brought a jug of iced water and patiently helped me to take a long, cool drink. Then she poured water on to a facecloth and wiped my face and arms with it to cool me down. Then she pushed the hair from my face, bent down and gently kissed my forehead, whispering, 'God bless, sleep well.' I felt that the nurse was my angel, sent by God to minister to me when I most needed the comfort.

In this passage Elijah is scared. He has run away and feels exhausted and unable to carry on. Then God sends an angel to care for him. He wakes up and finds food and drink that sustains him for the rest of his journey.

When we are at our lowest point God sends people to act as his angels to help us in whatever way we most need. Of course, that means that as his people, we need to be like angels to others, helping them in the same way.

Prayer: *Lord, thank you for the people who have ministered to me and brought me hope and consolation. Amen*

Thought for the day: To whom can I be an angel today?

Pam Lewis (Essex, England)

PRAYER FOCUS: THOSE AT THEIR LOWEST POINT

The gospel through deeds

Read 1 Corinthians 3:5–9

Let your light shine before others, that they may see your good deeds and glorify your Father in heaven.
Matthew 5:16 (NIV)

When I studied abroad at the Human Rights Institute in Strasbourg, France, I befriended students from Algeria and Tunisia. Since the programme focused on religious rights, we discussed religious freedom in our countries. We also talked about our personal religious beliefs. I used this opportunity to share my testimony: I was raised as an atheist in the USSR, but after Perestroika I accepted Jesus as my personal Saviour.

I also showed my faith through my deeds. The Bible teaches, 'Faith by itself, if it has no works, is dead' (James 2:17, NRSV). I assisted my new friends in their studies, shared my notes with them and helped them to cook dinner. I treated them with respect and our fellowship was cordial. I also prayed that Jesus' light would shine through me.

The apostle Paul wrote, 'I planted the seed, Apollos watered it, but God has been making it grow' (1 Corinthians 3:6). We can each do our part in sharing the good news – and trust the Lord to do the rest.

Prayer: *Dear Lord, help us to be doers of the word and not hearers only. In Jesus' name. Amen*

Thought for the day: My actions show my faith in God.

Tatiana Claudy (Indiana, US)

'Do you not care?'

Read Matthew 8:23–27

What manner of man is this, that even the winds and the sea obey him!

Matthew 8:27 (KJV)

Prior to elections in Kenya in 2017, we heard numerous appeals for a peaceful voting process. Even as the appeals for peace were being made, however, the fear of violence simmered deep within the voting citizens. Those fears were well founded as our country had experienced unprecedented electoral violence just a decade earlier.

As I thought of the fear we were experiencing, I remembered the disciples in the boat with Jesus, who were consumed with the fear of drowning in the sea. In the middle of a storm, they came to him, woke him up from sleep and said, 'Teacher, do you not care that we are perishing?' (Mark 4:38, NRSV). Jesus woke up, rebuked the storm and restored the disciples' peace. Jesus' actions reminded them and us that when we trust in Jesus, he will be with us through any circumstances. All we are required to do as children of the Most High God is to trust in him and his word and live in obedience to it. 'For with God nothing shall be impossible' (Luke 1:37, KJV).

Prayer: *Dear Lord, thank you for the peace you bring today. We look to you for help always. In the name of the Father, the Son and the Holy Spirit, we pray. Amen*

Thought for the day: Christ is the source of all peace.

Philip Polo (Nairobi, Kenya)

An unkindness of ravens

Read Psalm 94:17–19

When my anxieties multiply, your comforting calms me down.
Psalm 94:19 (CEB)

We were camping in Yellowstone National Park in Raven's Roost campground. When we were rudely awakened before dawn by a riotous chorus of caws, we learned why one term for a flock of ravens is an 'unkindness'.

I'm reminded of those ravens as I read the verse quoted above. It seems that worry invades us like a raucous unkindness of ravens cawing: 'You are doomed.' The disquieting mental noise of anxiety is almost impossible to ignore.

The psalmist says that God restores the peace and quiet: 'Your comforting calms me down.' God's word is full of promises that we can meditate on to bring comfort and peace to our minds. I love Zephaniah 3:17: 'The Lord your God is with you, the Mighty Warrior who saves. He will take great delight in you; in his love he will no longer rebuke you, but will rejoice over you with singing' (NIV). In place of the word 'you', I insert my name or the name of someone for whom I am praying. I celebrate the victory that God sees for my friends and me even when circumstances shout otherwise. When we delight in these promises, God restores peace to our souls.

Prayer: *God of peace, thank you for your powerful and comforting promises that chase away the ravens of worry. Amen*

Thought for the day: Trusting in God is my answer to worry.

Mark Weinrich (Nevada, US)

PRAYER FOCUS: SOMEONE OVERCOME BY WORRY

A walking testimony

Read 1 Peter 3:13–17

Let no one despise your youth, but set the believers an example in speech and conduct, in love, in faith, in purity.
1 Timothy 4:12 (NRSV)

As I watched Lainie, my 15-year-old granddaughter, walk out of school, I noticed that she was wearing a cross necklace and had John 3:16 printed on her T-shirt. On the way to drop off her friend Jeannie, I listened to the girls chat about an after-school Christian meeting and Lainie's church youth group. Then, Lainie reminded Jeannie to be ready for a lift to church on Sunday morning.

I compared Lainie's actions with my own at this same school years before. Although a Christian, I had been too worried about embarrassment or criticism to share my faith. And I hadn't done so in the years since. But that day, I resolved to follow Lainie's example. I prayed for help to overcome my fears. Soon, my simple acts – such as wearing a T-shirt with a Christian message, offering to pray with someone or comforting a hurting friend – prompted conversations about God's love. I found ways to encourage new worshippers, invite others to church and help with my church's many mission projects.

The more I risked, the more opportunities I had to witness to others. God calls each of us to spread the gospel, even if it means facing rejection or criticism. No matter our age or situation, God will lead us to serve others by showing them the way to Christ.

Prayer: *Dear God, give us courage and guidance to show others your love and grace. Amen*

Thought for the day: Today I will find ways to share God's word.

Nancy Lewis Shelton (Missouri, US)

Always a winner

Read Philippians 1:20–24

If we live, we live for the Lord; and if we die, we die for the Lord. So, whether we live or die, we belong to the Lord.
Romans 14:8 (NIV)

As my friend Charles waited for serious heart surgery, he had great peace. He explained, 'Whatever way it turns out, I'm a winner.' A few years later, he faced another heart procedure with the same peace and the same words.

When the apostle Paul wrote to the Christians in Rome, he told them that whether they lived or died they would always be with Jesus, and Jesus would always be with them. Eventually, Charles did pass from this world and went to be with the Lord. The truth of Charles' words provides comfort and a faithful example for me. Whenever any of us faces a trial, because of our faith in Christ, we can say, 'Whatever way it turns out, I'm a winner.'

Prayer: *Thank you, Lord, that you are always with us, whether in life or in death. We pray as Jesus taught us, saying, 'Our Father in heaven, hallowed be your name, your kingdom come, your will be done, on earth as it is in heaven. Give us today our daily bread. And forgive us our debts, as we also have forgiven our debtors. And lead us not into temptation, but deliver us from the evil one.'* Amen*

Thought for the day: No matter what I face today, Jesus is always with me.

Ted De Hass (Iowa, US)

PRAYER FOCUS: SOMEONE AWAITING HEART SURGERY
*Matthew 6:9–13

Losing focus

Read Matthew 14:22–33

Peter got down out of the boat, walked on the water and came towards Jesus. But when he saw the wind, he was afraid and, beginning to sink, cried out, 'Lord, save me!'
Matthew 14:29–30 (NIV)

One afternoon, I was standing on my paddleboard, looking into the clear water below. Suddenly, I saw a large, ominous shadow approaching. I strained to see what it was and began to slowly turn towards it. As I worried about the scary unknown, I lost my concentration on my paddleboarding technique and found myself submerged in deep water with my board flipped upside down. Worse yet, I no longer knew where the shadow was. Fearing a shark would sense my distress and attack, I tightly gripped the board as panic overcame me. I prayed, 'Help me, God!' Trying hard to trust in God's protection, I returned to shore unharmed.

Sometimes when I'm gliding across the water on my paddleboard I wonder what it was like for Peter to walk on the stormy sea. While focusing on Jesus, he was 'gliding' across the water as I do on my board. Then, when he focused on the threat, he lost sight of Jesus.

We all face many challenges throughout our lives – such as the death of loved ones, illness or job loss. These challenges can make us afraid, especially if we try to face them alone. Instead, we can confront them head-on through prayer and Bible study, and by seeking help from fellow Christians. I am always amazed at the peace God can provide during these trying times.

Prayer: *Dear God, our protector, help us to keep our focus on you so we won't sink into treacherous waters. Thank you for being with us. Amen*

Thought for the day: God hears me when I call for help and delivers me safely to the shore.

Ron Lazenby (Alabama, US)

A good Samaritan

Read Luke 10:25–37

[The lawyer] answered, 'You shall love the Lord your God with all your heart, and with all your soul, and with all your strength, and with all your mind; and your neighbour as yourself.'
Luke 10:27 (NRSV)

When I was a child, I enjoyed spending time in my father's tailoring shop, listening to him tell stories from his childhood while he worked. My father had a happy childhood in Armenia until war broke out in 1915. He was forced to flee from his home and he stayed on the move – walking by day, hiding among the trees by night.

One day while he was walking down a road, he saw a group of boys heading his way, intent on harming him because he was both Armenian and Christian. My father scrambled into a ditch, raised his arms and cried, 'Dear God, save me!' In desperation, he waved down a passing car. The driver stopped, told him to get into the car and asked, 'Where are you going?' My father stammered, 'Anywhere.'

The man took him to an inn and gave him fresh clothes. My father bathed, ate a good meal and slept at the inn that night. The following day my father wanted to thank the man, but the man was gone. He had paid for the night's stay and left some money for my father. Who was this man? My father never found out.

This stranger lived out the parable of the good Samaritan, caring for my father even though he didn't know him. We can all learn from the kindness that this man showed and remember that we have the ability to show love and mercy to others as well.

Prayer: *God of great mercy, thank you for watching over us in unexpected ways and through the people you send into our lives. Amen*

Thought for the day: Whom is God calling me to help today?

Rebeca Boyadjian (Montevideo, Uruguay)

Unity and harmony

Read Acts 2:1–11

How good and pleasant it is when God's people live together in unity!
Psalm 133:1 (NIV)

In our prison we have two choirs, one that sings in English and the other in Spanish. I am in the English choir. When there is a fifth Sunday in the month, we celebrate what we call 'Super Sunday', when the English and Spanish choirs join together to sing every song in both languages.

Our first Super Sunday became a powerful experience when we all sang together in harmony. During the service, both choirs surrounded the congregation while singing 'We Give You All' or 'Recibe'. Those who felt called to pray did so. I got down on my knees, put my face to the ground and felt the Holy Spirit surround me as I prayed. When I had finished praying, I stood and looked across the congregation. What I saw amazed me. As I looked from person to person, I knew that Jesus was smiling and loving his church.

In the scripture quoted above, the psalmist says it is good and pleasant when God's people live in unity. When believers come together in love to worship, the connection and unity that we experience are powerful. Jesus' love unifies believers and creates harmony. Whether we are at church, at work, at home or even in prison, we can be encouraged by the power of worshipping as one.

Prayer: *Dear God, help us to live and worship together in harmony today and every day. Amen*

Thought for the day: The Holy Spirit brings us together in harmony.

Steven Paul Simmons (Texas, US)

Never in vain

Read Romans 1:8–17
Let us not become weary in doing good, for at the proper time we will reap a harvest if we do not give up.
Galatians 6:9 (NIV)

'Hi. It's Bonnie,' said the voice on the phone. 'I just wanted you to know that I've come back to the Lord.' The ring of excitement in her voice when she said these words identified her as the person who had once attended a Bible study I'd taught. Bonnie asked if she could come over to my house to tell me more.

That afternoon, her voice rang with joy as she told me of her ministry with people new to Canada. 'And you won't believe this, but I'm helping with a ladies' Bible study.' Women from many countries now gather in her living room to study God's word.

Bonnie's story warmed my heart and reminded me that the time and energy I had spent in our Bible study mattered. When things or people don't turn out as we'd hoped, we may feel as if our work has been in vain. We may even become discouraged and give up. But that day, I learned that nothing we do in the name of Jesus is meaningless. If we do not lose heart and give up, then someday, when we've forgotten our efforts or written them off as a loss, our 'reward' may just ring the doorbell and tell us stories of grace that will fill our hearts with praise.

Prayer: *Dear Lord, help us to stay faithful in the work you've given us, always remembering its eternal value. Amen*

Thought for the day: My efforts for the Lord are never in vain.

Rose McCormick Brandon (Ontario, Canada)

A new creation

Read Psalm 127:1–5
See, I am making all things new.
Revelation 21:5 (NRSV)

My two guides and translators, Kaarel and Taavet, made my visit to Tallinn, Estonia, comfortable and convenient. One day our tour included a great open-air theatre where music festivals are held, a drive past the presidential residence and a visit to the museum. As we concluded our tour, Kaarel said, 'We are near a house built in the early 1930s that my brother is restoring. Why don't we drive by and see how things are going?'

As we drove down the tree-lined avenue, I noticed the roofline of a very interesting house – it turned out to be the house we were to visit! I was enthralled by its condition: it was so sturdy and well built. I thought of the words of Jesus: 'See, I am making all things new.' The owner was stripping away all that was useless and beginning with new windows, a new heating system and plans to create a totally new house. I remarked how thrilling it would be to see the completed project.

Then I thought how Jesus Christ had transformed my own life. I am not all I can be, but Christ is changing me into a new creation. I will never be the same.

Prayer: *Dear Lord Jesus, help us to understand that we are still under construction. Give us patience and courage to embrace the new life you offer. Amen*

Thought for the day: My creator is not yet finished making me.

W. David Lewis (Tennessee, US)

A snake, a Bible and me

Read Lamentations 3:22–26

Your word is a lamp for my feet, a light on my path.
Psalm 119:105 (NIV)

Every morning that summer it was just me, my Bible and a snake. I had flown 750 miles across the country to work at a young people's summer camp. While it was a remarkable place, I couldn't shake the feeling of loneliness. On the outside, I was the typical camp worker – wearing a smile from sunrise to sundown. But the truth was, I had never wanted so badly to go home.

And yet, when I felt emptiest, God blessed me through a piece of paper someone gave me shortly before I arrived: a list of 100 verses of scripture to memorise.

Every dawn I would wake up before the campers, and walk to find the same spot at the edge of the lake. I would unfold the list, welcome the snake who had moseyed to the rock opposite me and open my Bible. Never have I had a more peaceful, life-lifting time with God.

Often since then those verses have popped into my mind – relieving me from anxiety, holding me back from temptation, guiding me towards a solution, reminding me to pray. Recalling those hours with God has been a constant reminder of the peace only he can provide.

Prayer: *Dear God, thank you for meeting us today and every day. We need you more than the bread we eat and the air we breathe. Amen*

Thought for the day: God is good to me – all the time.

Melissa Ferguson (Tennessee, US)

God cares for all of us

Read Matthew 7:7–12

Give us today our daily bread.
Matthew 6:11 (NIV)

Our daughter-in-law and four-year-old granddaughter were travelling from Mexico to Tokyo during the approach of Hurricane Harvey. They were scheduled to take a connecting flight out of Houston, Texas, but due to the bad weather the airport closed shortly after their arrival in Houston. Stranded, they took a taxi to seek shelter at a hotel.

Thankfully, their hotel did not suffer as much damage as others in the area, but because of the emergency, food supplies were scarce. My wife and I were deeply concerned for them. Each time we ate a meal, we prayed that God would provide for the needs of our daughter-in-law and granddaughter. God did provide sustenance for them, using other people to care for them. Finally, after ten days, they were able to continue their journey, healthy and safe.

When we ask God to give us today our daily bread, we recognise that he is our provider and we can trust that he will supply what we need. Especially when our situation feels hopeless, we can put our faith in God.

Prayer: *Loving God, we give thanks for the blessings you provide for us, and we pray for those who are facing difficult times. We trust your providence. Amen*

Thought for the day: I will trust God to provide for me today and every day.

José Vergara (Puebla, Mexico)

Restore point

Read 2 Corinthians 5:15–21

If anyone is in Christ, the new creation has come: the old has gone, the new is here!

2 Corinthians 5:17 (NIV)

This morning, my computer was not working properly. It's old, so I'm patient with it, but the screen saver was suddenly different, and all of my emails had disappeared. I remembered that our son had shown me how to create a 'restore point', a technique to restore settings on a computer to a prior time. So I did that; my screen saver was restored to the current version – and the emails reappeared!

I sometimes wish for a 'restore point' in my personal life. Relationships that once were good can go sour with a single negative encounter that leads to bitterness, resentment and division. I long to go back to when a relationship was positive, good and satisfying.

God does that for us. Through his death and resurrection, Christ reconciled us, bringing us into communion with him. When I mess things up with a negative word or act or thought, ugliness builds like a darkening sky on a stormy day. But God's grace is always there, able to restore my spirit to a place of peace, hope and love. I can choose to confess my wrongdoing to the other person and to God, then ask for forgiveness and for God's help to see the good in the person I am at odds with. Often for me, this is a daily process to restore communion with others and with God. Thanks to his grace, I can choose to be restored.

Prayer: *Dear Lord, help us to keep our hearts pure and clean towards you and towards others. Amen*

Thought for the day: God's grace is always available to help me make a fresh start.

Susan Parr (Indiana, US)

Confidence in God

Read Joshua 1:1–9

The Sovereign Lord is my strength; he makes my feet like the feet of a deer, he enables me to tread on the heights.
Habakkuk 3:19 (NIV)

A few years ago, I volunteered with a disaster relief organisation. Even though my background was in social work, part of my job was to get supplies from local hardware stores for the construction sites. During my training I was dropped off at a hardware store with a two-page list of items to find. I had no clue what some of these items were, so my first reaction was fear. I saw three ways to respond. One was to let self-pity and doubt overwhelm me: 'I should never have taken this position. I don't know what I am doing. I will look like a fool doing it.' The second response could be anger: 'Why is this organisation making me do this? They should know I don't know what these items are.' Or third, I could respond with a confident attitude – confidence not in myself but in God.

I had no clue what I was doing but God did. After all, the Lord said, 'I will lead the blind by ways they have not known, along unfamiliar paths I will guide them... I will not forsake them' (Isaiah 42:16). I knew that God had called me to do this work, so I chose the third response.

Whenever challenges come our way, we can choose to trust God. On our own we may be lost, but with him we can handle any problem. God is always faithful.

Prayer: *Dear Lord, thank you for your wisdom and guidance. Amen*

Thought for the day: Because God is with me, I can be confident.

Melissa Wilson (Pennsylvania, US)

Our Father's business

Read Luke 2:41–52

[Jesus] said unto them, How is it that ye sought me? [Know] ye not that I must be about my Father's business?
Luke 2:49 (KJV)

My father taught his children many valuable lessons – the foremost being that we were to revere the name of God at all times and to honour the love and unity of our family. From the time I was very young, he seemed to place a great amount of trust in me. In the safe and secure environment of our little town, he would send me to the bank to deposit sums of cash from the sales generated at his place of business. Within two months of my 16th birthday and once I received my driving licence, my father allowed me to drive 120 miles to pick up supplies from the headquarters of his company. It felt good to 'be about my father's business', to represent him in what I thought to be important affairs.

For years now, I have also represented my heavenly Father's business, the most important in the world. It amazes me that God entrusts the affairs and cares of the human soul to us disciples. Though for years I preached sermons with words from the pulpits of churches, today I preach with my daily words and actions.

Prayer: *Father God, teach us to be trustworthy in serving you as we serve others. Amen*

Thought for the day: Every day I can deliver God's love and grace to a weary world.

Wil I. Jackson (North Carolina, US)

Opportunity

Read John 14:23–27

[Jesus said,] 'Peace I leave with you.'
John 14:27 (NIV)

'Grandma, we've got a problem!' That's my grandson Cesare's favourite phrase. At this point I remind him that we have an opportunity for God to find a solution. Problems do indeed arise, seemingly every day. But the choice of how we handle them is ours. We can either allow fear to well up on the inside, or we can take our problems to the Lord. The sooner we turn them over to God, the sooner we'll receive his peace.

In John 14, Jesus said that he came to give us peace. He knew the imperfections in our world, and he knew that we could never handle them on our own. He also knew that every day each one of us will face something that will require his help. That's why Jesus said that the peace he gives us is not like what the world tries to give. The world's peace is superficial. Although it may suppress our problems for the moment, it's not lasting.

So today the choice is ours. What will we do the next time a problem arises? Will we dwell on the problem? Or will we make a conscious choice to turn it over to God?

Prayer: *Dear God, help us remember to call on you for the problems and fears we face. In the name of the Prince of Peace, Jesus Christ. Amen*

Thought for the day: With God's help I can view challenges as opportunities.

Del Bates (Florida, US)

Sowing God's word

Read Romans 11:33–36
Oh, the depth of the riches of the wisdom and knowledge of God!
Romans 11:33 (NIV)

In my retirement I have taken on the challenge of distributing New Testaments to people I meet. One day, I visited a friend who wanted me to read to him from the Bible. On my way home, I met three teen-age boys. I offered one of them a New Testament, but he refused. 'I don't need that stuff!' he scoffed. This was my first effort to give away one of the New Testaments I had brought with me, so I was disappointed. Some minutes later I met another boy of about the same age. He received my gift with a broad smile and said, 'Thank you!' He even gave me a hug. Later in the afternoon I met two young women from Lithuania, who happened to know my Norwegian language. They were each happy to get a copy of the New Testament.

These experiences have made me think about the words from Ecclesiastes 11:6: 'Sow your seed in the morning, and at evening let your hands not be idle, for you do not know which will succeed, whether this or that, or whether both will do equally well.'

There is always time and opportunity for us to sow the seed of the gospel. We may have disappointments, but we will also receive great blessings.

Prayer: *Dear Lord, thank you for giving us different ways to serve you. Help us to follow where you lead us. Amen*

Thought for the day: We can give no greater gift than the word of God.

Anne-Lise Aure (Sunnmøre, Norway)

Now is the time

Read Luke 18:1–8

Be on your guard; stand firm in the faith; be courageous; be strong.
Do everything in love.
1 Corinthians 16:13–14 (NIV)

The person who teaches a Bible class with me is always proclaiming what a great era we are living in. Some people readily agree, but a few roll their eyes as if to say, 'Doesn't he read the papers that report on the turmoil we live in?' We are surrounded by reports of wars, political unrest, identity thefts, disease, abuse, drugs and persecution of Christians in certain parts of the world. This could lead us to believe that the world is falling apart.

When the world sees uncertainty and chaos, isn't it possible for the church and individual Christians to see opportunity? What better time to proclaim to the world a God we can depend on? We need only to read scripture and know that God is in control. Jesus explains in Luke 18:6–8 that those who cry out to God will get justice, and then, wanting to spur the listeners to greater faith, he asks, 'When the Son of Man comes, will he find faith on the earth?' Just imagine how much we can do! Now is the time for Christians to live their faith.

Prayer: *God of justice, help us to be more like your Son and to stand firm in sharing the gospel with the world. Amen*

Thought for the day: No matter what is going on around me, I will stand steadfast for Christ.

Walter N. Maris (Missouri, US)

Active participation

Read Revelation 3:15–22
Because you are lukewarm – neither hot nor cold – I am about to spit you out of my mouth.
Revelation 3:16 (NIV)

As I arrived at the gym in January, I noticed many new faces – people armed with their New Year's resolutions to get fit. But as I did my usual exercise routine, I noticed that some of these new people were just sitting on the weight machines looking at their phones rather than actively moving – as if just spending time in a gym would make them physically fitter.

Don't we sometimes approach our spiritual walk with God in the same way? We may own a nice Bible but not read it. We may join an outreach programme but not take on any tasks to contribute. We may go to church every Sunday but just sit there expecting the choir and the minister to put in all the effort for us. Scripture tells us that we are not to be lukewarm in our faith.

Our walk with God is an active process and requires time, attention and full participation. Others cannot do the work for us. Rather than being lukewarm we need to be fully invested in our quest to be more like Jesus. The rewards are immense – and eternal.

Prayer: *Dear Lord, stir up our desire to be closer to you and to actively work so that our relationship with you grows and develops. Amen*

Thought for the day: God wants our active participation.

Margaret Anderson (Kansas, US)

Finding rest

Read Psalm 77:1–12

I remembered my songs in the night.
Psalm 77:6 (NIV)

My wife, Mercy, lay on the hospital bed, struggling with severe pain from the cancer cells that had spread through her body. Even in her pain, however, she enjoyed hearing and singing Christian songs. She rested her head on the pillow as she listened to her music, and also prayed for her fellow patients.

Mercy particularly liked to sing one song, which invites us to come to Jesus when we are weary and lean on Jesus to rest. She told me that she found great comfort leaning on Jesus – just as the song said. On 17 September 2005, she held my hand as her breathing slowed and she entered her heavenly home for eternal rest.

Even though her death created a void for me and my loved ones, I thank God for Mercy's witness. She could remain calm and sing even when she passed through her deepest darkness. Such a faithful witness was the result of her experience of leaning on Jesus. Her life and death continue to give hope to all who knew her.

Prayer: *Dear Lord Jesus, we pray for all who suffer from deadly diseases. Be with them as they pass through the valley of deepest darkness. Enable them to lean on you and find rest. Amen*

Thought for the day: When we are weary, we can lean on Jesus.

T.G. Johnson (Kerala, India)

More than skin-deep

Read Proverbs 31:10–30

Charm is deceptive, and beauty is fleeting; but a woman who fears the Lord is to be praised.
Proverbs 31:30 (NIV)

Lately when I look in the mirror, I notice the inevitable signs of ageing. It is hard to accept in a culture where we are bombarded with adverts for expensive skincare products that promise we will be 'ageless' if we use them. Celebrities who spend vast amounts of money and time to look younger are offered as ideals of beauty. It's no wonder many of us feel bad about how we look on the outside.

But we serve a God who loves us for what's on the inside and wants us to love ourselves as well. And when we focus on what God loves in us, we will find true joy. God tells us just the opposite of what the world says, that our spiritual selves are more important than what is on the outside.

No one is truly ageless. In fact, all of us will perish one day. But what's on the inside will shine before others as we share Christ with them; and that same Spirit will carry us into eternal life.

Prayer: *Dear Lord, help us to remember that the way we reflect the image of Christ can influence everyone around us. Help us to reflect your love to others as we pray, 'Father, hallowed be your name, your kingdom come. Give us each day our daily bread. Forgive us our sins, for we also forgive everyone who sins against us. And lead us not into temptation.'* Amen*

Thought for the day: God is more interested in what's in my heart than how I look.

Jenny McBride (Alabama, US)

PRAYER FOCUS: SOMEONE STRUGGLING WITH BODY IMAGE
*Luke 11:2–4

Whose world?

Read Revelation 21:1–7

In the beginning God created the heavens and the earth.
Genesis 1:1 (NIV)

Many people want to 'make our world a better place'. This may be through litter-picking, working to reduce our use of plastic or lobbying for an end to food waste. All are worthy things to do: God instructed the first human beings to be good stewards of the created world.

When war and famine and terrorism bombard our TV screens we may become anxious and tempted to despair. But it helps us to remember that the world doesn't belong to us; it belongs to God and he is in control. My father once wrote a letter to his children in which he said, 'Our lives are not ruled by random chance but by a loving heavenly Father.' It was a belief that sustained him through a long life, and which he passed on to his children and grandchildren.

As we work at being good stewards of our world, let us trust God in all our circumstances, acknowledging that he, who began all things, will restore his world and make all things new.

Prayer: *Thank you, almighty God, for your beautiful world. Help us to care for its beauty and be worthy stewards of all the good things that we see around us. Amen*

Thought for the day: God is in control of his world.

Pam Pointer (Wiltshire, England)

Limited vision

Read Psalm 78:9–16

I will instruct you and teach you in the way you should go; I will counsel you with my loving eye on you.
Psalm 32:8 (NIV)

After breakfast, my husband, daughter and I hurried to the observation car of the train, eager to see the way ahead. The side and back windows were all clear, allowing us to watch the steep rock faces, lakes and forests – and even passing trains. We could also see the track behind us. But the iced-over front window kept us from seeing the way ahead.

In my disappointment I thought about the twists and turns of life that prevent me from seeing where I am going. It reminded me of the Israelites when they left Egypt, heading for the promised land (Exodus 12—14). They did not know the way. What's more, at one point the Red Sea blocked the path before them and the Egyptians closed in behind them. Yet God never left them alone – parting the sea and then leading them with a pillar of cloud by day and a pillar of fire by night (see Exodus 13:22).

God had a plan for the people and asked for their trust in being led safely to the promised land. On that train trip, I needed to trust that the driver had a clear view through their window so that we would arrive at our destination. In life, our vision is limited, which can make our way seem treacherous, but we can trust our God who knows the way.

Prayer: *Dear God, when the path ahead is not clear, help us to trust you to lead us safely to our destination. Amen*

Thought for the day: God knows the way and will lead me forward.

Carol Harrison (Saskatchewan, Canada)

Like flowers in the field

Read Matthew 6:25–34

The desert and the parched land will be glad; the wilderness will rejoice and blossom. Like the crocus, it will burst into bloom; it will rejoice greatly and shout for joy… They will see the glory of the Lord, the splendour of our God.

Isaiah 35:1–2 (NIV)

As I was walking with my mother this morning, we noticed lilies growing among the overgrown grass and weeds in a site that has been abandoned since Hurricane Katrina in 2005. It was both striking and touching to see an example of such beauty in the midst of such ugliness. It brought to my mind the words of Jesus telling us not to worry about what we shall wear or eat because God knows what we need and will provide it for us.

In the same way that my mother and I could not see the bulb underground being nourished, eventually to become a beautiful flower, we may not notice when God is hard at work in our lives. But much like a flower in bloom, the beauty and splendour of the end result will be visible to all.

Prayer: *Dear God, thank you for being a steadfast presence of love in our lives. Help us to trust that you are at work even when we cannot see it. In the name of Jesus, we pray. Amen*

Thought for the day: Though we may not know it, God is always at work in our lives.

Patrick Castleberry (Mississippi, US)

PRAYER FOCUS: THOSE STRUGGLING TO FEEL GOD'S PRESENCE

Showing honour

Read Ephesians 4:29–32
Love one another with mutual affection; outdo one another in showing honour.
Romans 12:10 (NRSV)

'You're a good man, Bert.' My husband looked at me in surprise. After the morning we'd had, he didn't expect to hear these words – at least not until he'd spent more time in the doghouse. Even though I wasn't feeling a lot of love and admiration for my husband at that moment, I knew he loved me, and I didn't want my unforgiving attitude to damage our relationship.

It was incredible how quickly our day improved once I changed my attitude. Every time I choose to honour Bert rather than chiding him about something or giving him the silent treatment, I feel better about him, myself and our marriage. I'm sure he feels the same way when he responds kindly after I've been unkind to him. From what I've heard from others, I know we're not the only people who could benefit from today's quoted verse. I especially love the part, 'outdo one another in showing honour'.

Rather than keeping score with our spouse, sibling, colleague or friend, we can instead ask God to show us new ways to love and honour those around us – especially on the days when they need affection and respect the most.

Prayer: *Dear Lord, help us to show honour and to affirm those around us today. Amen*

Thought for the day: Honouring others changes the course of my day.

Sheryl H. Boldt (Florida, US)

God does the rest

Read 1 Peter 4:10–11

Do not fear, for I am with you; do not be dismayed, for I am your God.
I will strengthen you and help you; I will uphold you with my righteous
right hand.
Isaiah 41:10 (NIV)

My good friend Fred has taught me a lot about serving the Lord. Fred started his career as a secondary school teacher but was troubled by seeing hurting students making poor life choices. He felt a calling to do something to help. After much prayer with his wife, Dorothy, Fred resigned from teaching and started a ministry to help at-risk young people find a life with Jesus Christ. That leap of faith 38 years ago has helped thousands of at-risk teenagers, and the ministry still thrives today.

After ensuring a successful leadership handover, Fred 'retired' from the youth ministry; but he hadn't finished serving. In 2004 he started a second ministry to help ex-prisoners make the challenging adjustment back into society. Like the youth ministry, the focus is on a personal relationship with Christ, and the ministry is still going strong today.

I once asked Fred what motivated Dorothy and him to be such faithful servants for the Lord. He humbly replied, 'We just said yes. God did the rest.' What a great reminder that God doesn't require us to be special or talented. We just need to say yes, and God can do the rest.

Prayer: *Dear God, thank you for never leaving us no matter what we encounter. Help us to be humble servants for your kingdom, always trusting in you. In Jesus' name. Amen*

Thought for the day: When I say yes, God will do the rest.

John D. Bown (Minnesota, US)

Don't be afraid

Read 2 Kings 6:8–23

[Elisha] replied, 'Do not be afraid, for there are more with us than there are with them.'
2 Kings 6:16 (NRSV)

We opened a school for children in a mountain village. One day, a group of people came to our house, wanting to close the school. One of our children ran up and said, 'Mum, there are a lot of people coming to our house, shouting. What should we do, Mum? Call the police!' But then our youngest child said, 'Let us pray, Mum.' We joined hands in prayer to the Lord Jesus.

Soon a rainstorm began. The area in front of our house flooded, but the flood did not come into our yard. Most of the people in front of the house disbanded and ran away. Only three of their leaders remained at the front of our house.

Our youngest child's response reminds me of Elisha when he was surrounded by his enemies. While his servant responded with fear, Elisha prayed for God's help. Remembering what Elisha did, we invited the three chilly leaders into our house. We gave them a change of clothes and provided hot tea and food for them. One of them asked, 'Why do you treat us so well?' I replied, 'Because God loves you and wants us to do all this for you.' When the rain stopped, the people apologised and left our house.

May we remember that God is greater than anyone and can free us from fear.

Prayer: *Dear God, thank you for your protection of us each day. Help us trust you and give our fears to you. Amen*

Thought for the day: When I am afraid, I will pray and trust God.

Linda Chandra (Banten, Indonesia)

From worry to joy

Read Psalm 40:1–3

[Jesus said,] 'I've said these things to you so that you will have peace in me. In the world you have distress. But be encouraged! I have conquered the world.'
John 16:33 (CEB)

During my afternoon walks, I enjoy listening to the birds sing, watching the trees sway in the wind and hearing the buzz of activity. However, on this afternoon, the rain poured down and my eyes were focused on the road. I had never noticed the cracks in the road or the occasional pot-hole. I felt I needed to watch my every step for fear of stumbling. Then my neighbour Mark drove up and rolled down his window to offer me a lift home, out of the rain. With just a few words from my neighbour, I no longer thought about the obstacles in my path. Instead, my thoughts were of Mark's kindness.

Sometimes stress and the troubles of life are like the rain, keeping us from looking up and seeing God's blessings. Instead, we focus only on our problems.

Maybe today we can share a kind word and help someone look up from their difficulties to find joy and peace in God.

Prayer: *Dear God, when we are burdened with the stress of this world, help us to realise that you are the great comforter. Amen*

Thought for the day: When I share a kind word, I show the love of Christ.

Randy Jennings (Virginia, US)

Like a forest

Read Romans 15:1–7

Accept one another… just as Christ accepted you, in order to bring praise to God.

Romans 15:7 (NIV)

As my husband and I drove through the forest to our campsite, I studied the trees along the road. One had some dead branches, another a broken top; still others had bent limbs or odd shapes. In fact, every tree seemed to have some imperfection – yet together they formed a vibrant, green forest full of life. They provided shade for ferns and orchids and homes for any number of animals – from tiger swallowtail butterflies to white-tailed deer. And they gave us a peaceful place to camp and enjoy nature. Even the dead trees had a specific purpose: they were rotting into compost to nourish younger plants.

That forest reminded me of the people who make up God's church. We all have scars and imperfections. We make mistakes. Yet together we can form something beautiful. We can bring forgiveness to the broken, strengthen the tempted and pick up the fallen so that they – in turn – can do the same for us. Instead of condemning those who make mistakes, we can offer a listening ear and a helping hand. Together we can become a community that serves God and helps those in need while strengthening one another.

Prayer: *Dear God, help us to accept others and love them as you do, despite their imperfections – and despite our own. Amen*

Thought for the day: Though we are scarred and imperfect, God builds the church with us.

Susan Thogerson Maas (Oregon, US)

Church at its best

When I was an undergraduate, I went to a Christian university that required students to attend chapel each day. Often chapel services felt like an obligation and an interruption to my day – time that could be spent doing something else. I attended because I had to, and when it was over I would quickly move on with my day. I had my doubts about whether I belonged in the community at all and sometimes wondered if I wouldn't be better off somewhere else.

Then one morning, the family members of a teacher who had died attended our chapel service. As a gesture of our encouragement and support, we sang to the family. In my church tradition, singing 'psalms and hymns and spiritual songs' (Ephesians 5:19, NRSV) is a significant aspect of the worship service, and we do it well. I love to sing, and I love much of the music that is part of my church tradition. It was a good moment for me and a good one for my faith community. It is still difficult to describe what happened in that moment, but something sacred and powerful occurred that still sustains me today.

Were someone to ask me what keeps me active and involved in my church community, what keeps me a faithful churchgoer in moments of doubt, what encourages me and gives me strength when I fail, I would tell them about that morning in chapel when I was a college student. My church community came together to show love and support for people who were experiencing a great tragedy and all the grief and pain such an event brings. To me that moment was church at its best.

I admit that in the years since, in church on Sunday I have sometimes had the same doubts that I had when I was a student: do I belong here? Would I be better off somewhere else? I have moments when I am frustrated with church, and I want to give up. I become so focused on everything that is going wrong that I lose sight of everything that is going right. Sometimes it's hard for me to see beyond the ways we treat one another – the words we speak without thinking or the needs of others we overlook because we have become bogged down in minutiae.

When I grow weary with my church community, I go back to that moment in chapel when I was a college student. It reminds me of all that is good about church and that we are at our best when we are caring for one another and loving, supporting and encouraging each other along the way. As the writer of the letter to the Hebrews says, 'Let us consider how we may spur one another on towards love and good deeds, not giving up meeting together, as some are in the habit of doing, but encouraging one another – and all the more as you see the Day approaching' (10:24–25, NIV). I remain grateful to my fellow Christians who have helped me along the way, especially in my moments of weakness, frustration or doubt. I remain grateful for that moment in chapel and how it has kept me going.

Our church communities don't always get it right. This has been the case for a long time, as we see when we read Paul's letters. But much of the time church communities do get it right; and at those times, I believe that we get it very right. The times when we are most like Christ in our thoughts and actions are what nourish me the most. I think this is true for all of us. Though we mess up sometimes – individually and collectively – this doesn't have to discourage us from trying to be more Christlike each day. So let us love, support and encourage one another along the way. Let us not give up when frustrations and doubts creep in, but show love and compassion to others every chance we get. We never know what difference it could make.

Several meditations in this issue address Christian community. You may want to read again the meditations for 2, 18, 22, 26, 30 May; 5, 9, 10, 19, 23, 30 June; 1, 11 and 21 July and 24 August before responding to the reflection questions below.

QUESTIONS FOR REFLECTION

1 When have you experienced frustration or doubt in your church community? How did you deal with your frustration or doubt?

2 Give an example from your own church community that shows Christian love, support and encouragement at its best.

Andrew Garland Breeden
Acquisitions Editor

Not only me

Read Exodus 17:9–13

When Moses' hands grew tired… Aaron and Hur held his hands up – one on one side, one on the other – so that his hands remained steady till sunset.

Exodus 17:12 (NIV)

During my last year at high school, I coordinated the singing groups at our church and volunteered for our ministry to the homeless. I gave guitar lessons to children and played the piano for another church's choir practice on Wednesday nights. And when our church was without a minister for several months, I decided to do whatever I could to help keep things going. But like Moses, my arms were getting tired.

I had become caught in the illusion that all of this was my responsibility alone. Too many times through the years I've thought that God wanted me to hold things up all on my own. But I was forgetting that though God can use me, he will never use only me. Even Moses needed Aaron and Hur to help him hold up the staff; I was trying to hold up too many ministries all on my own.

I wanted to be the one who did everything for God, but that wasn't possible for me or what he expected of me. None of us can sustain God's work alone; instead we are blessed with our community of faith. If we can learn to lean on the Lord and the church, together we can accomplish truly amazing things.

Prayer: *Dear Lord, open us to accept the help of others to do the good work that you have called us to do. Amen*

Thought for the day: How can I rely on others to help me do God's work?

Cameron Catanzano (California, US)

Seeds of compassion

Read Colossians 3:1–12

As God's chosen people, holy and dearly loved, clothe yourselves with compassion, kindness, humility, gentleness and patience.
Colossians 3:12 (NIV)

As I sat in the waiting area of the hospital, my thoughts were fixed on my asthma-related breathing issues. I had not planned to spend time at the hospital that day. Nearby sat a five-year-old boy named Dominic, who had a small bandage on his head. His mother confided that he was quite frightened. I edged over to the open seat next to Dominic and asked him if he would like to see some animal photos on my mobile phone. As my attention shifted from myself to the boy, I quickly had a new friend.

Soon Dominic noticed an elderly woman quietly crying on the opposite side of the waiting room. 'Would you like to come with me to check on her?' I asked. As I expressed Dominic's concern to her, she introduced herself and shook his hand. Before long, she and Dominic were looking at pictures of her pet dogs and grandchildren. I smiled as the kindness in both their hearts overtook their immediate worries.

My interaction with Dominic helped me to realise that we can allow God's kindness to travel with us wherever we go. As we plant seeds of compassion, they are multiplied exponentially. And in each action and word – to God be the glory!

Prayer: *God of compassion, thank you for your daily compassion. May we seek opportunities to extend your love and grace to those around us. Amen*

Thought for the day: God's love and kindness can shine through me to others who are suffering.

Lin Daniels (Massachusetts, US)

Taking a risk

Read Matthew 5:11–16

Let your light so shine before men, that they may see your good works, and glorify your Father which is in heaven.
Matthew 5:16 (KJV)

At the age of 19 I felt God gently nudging me to join a mission organisation where I would attend a full-time discipleship training school. I was longing to discover the God I said I had known for the previous ten years, and this seemed just the ticket. I was ready to give up everything for this opportunity, but no one else in my life agreed with me. They said, 'How do you know it is God nudging you?' and 'You have a great job!' and 'What will you do after that?' Everyone had questions that seemed to imply that they thought I had lost my mind.

But I had peace in my heart about this idea, and I knew it had come from God. That was all I needed to hold on to when nothing else seemed to make sense. Following God's guidance leaves me happier and more fulfilled. When I'm at peace with my choices and I'm following God's will, my light shines. Other people see it and ask what I'm doing right.

To make ourselves available to God, we sometimes have to take risks. Sometimes those risks take us out of our comfort zone. But it's in the dimness of the uncomfortable unknown that our lights shine best!

Prayer: *Dear God, help us to be ready to go where you call us and to trust your guidance so that our lights will shine before others. Amen*

Thought for the day: Even if others question me, I will be ready to answer God's call.

Amorelle Reneisha Browne (Grenada)

Rejoice, pray, give thanks

Read 1 Thessalonians 5:12–24

Rejoice always, pray continually, give thanks in all circumstances; for this is God's will for you in Christ Jesus.

1 Thessalonians 5:16–18 (NIV)

I have been a Christian for over 40 years and have studied and meditated on 1 Thessalonians several times. Though I have often slowed down and considered every phrase of the verses quoted above, it wasn't until my youngest son was deployed overseas that I began truly to comprehend the depth and breadth of Paul's words.

When a loved one is in harm's way, you find yourself praying while brushing your hair, while driving, during lunchtime. Finding myself in a constant state of prayer was a new stage in my relationship with Christ. He is always there, but how often do we take the opportunity to reach out to him in prayer? Now that my son has returned safely – though he is going back again next year – I realise anew that, although we have done our part in raising him, he belongs to the Lord. Meanwhile I will take advantage of the countless opportunities to go to my Lord and Saviour in prayer.

Prayer: *Heavenly Father, we praise you for hearing and answering our prayers. Help us to continue in steadfast prayer throughout each day. Amen*

Thought for the day: I will rejoice with prayerful thanksgiving today and always.

Ted Whitford (California, US)

Created to create

Read Genesis 1:20–27
God created humankind in his image.
Genesis 1:27 (NRSV)

At Honolulu Zoo, my husband and I laughed at grey birds with pink faces that made them look as if they were blushing. We marvelled at red, green and yellow parrots that squawked from the trees. When I saw a blue bird with a crest that looked like a fancy hat, I thought about the way that humans were created in God's own image.

We create clothing as colourful as God made birds' feathers. We use the trees God made to create tables and houses. Pictures of God's beautiful world adorn our walls. When I watch TV or scroll through social media sites, I usually come away feeling unsatisfied. But when I create a delicious dinner for my family or paint a picture, I feel fulfilled.

Our creative God made us to be creative beings. When we create something – plant a garden, sing a song or make a hat – we're happier because we're fulfilling God's purpose for us. The possibilities for creativity are as big as the world that God created for us to enjoy.

Prayer: *Dear God, give us ideas and confidence to use the creativity you gave us to make our lives and the lives of others more interesting and joyful. Amen*

Thought for the day: God made me a creative being.

Janet Asbridge (Washington, US)

True light

Read Psalm 34:1–8

[God] comforts us in all our troubles, so that we can comfort those in any trouble with the comfort we ourselves receive from God.
2 Corinthians 1:4 (NIV)

While undergoing medical treatment, I suffered a severe bout of depression. After the crisis had passed, I centred my thoughts on my heavenly Father whose care and presence were steadfast during those difficult days. I thanked God for my family, who helped me by demonstrating unconditional love and strength. I gave thanks for the doctors, for the medication and for the people who prayed for my healing and recuperation. Most of all, I thanked God for sustaining me when I was incapable of sustaining myself.

Throughout this experience, I have been reassured of my capacity to guide and encourage other people in their own times of crisis in my work as a college chaplain. What a privilege it is to serve God! What a great responsibility it is to guide others to Jesus! Motivated by the Holy Spirit to proclaim the good news of salvation, I am humbled to know that in the midst of a crisis we can still be channels of blessing to others.

Prayer: *Great healer, thank you for shining your light and guiding us out of the depths of distress. Your love is our recovery and sustaining life source. Amen*

Thought for the day: God can transform a crisis into an opportunity to serve.

Luciria Aguirre Naranjo (Cali, Colombia)

Time remaining

Read Ephesians 5:15–17

Teach us to count our days that we may gain a wise heart.
Psalm 90:12 (NRSV)

In my youth, summer seemed to last forever. Now I am past the age of 65, that's not the case anymore. I'm particularly aware of the way time passes when I ride an exercise bike at my local gym. A monitor on the bike gives me all kinds of information. But I'm focused on two categories: time elapsed and time remaining.

Today's reading from Ephesians reminds me to live wisely, 'making the most of the time' (v. 16). When I think about the time elapsed in my life, I know I haven't been very wise. Perhaps that is why I want to focus my remaining time in life on the things God needs me to do in the future.

How do I accomplish this? To start with, I must fully comprehend that time is a blink in the whirlwind of life. God will send me opportunities, but if I make excuses, then I will miss the chance to help people in need. Time is ticking. From now on, instead of hesitating, I will listen to God and get busy.

Prayer: *Heavenly Father, help us to be wise in using our time for your good. Amen*

Thought for the day: I will make the most of the time God has given me.

William Avery Pike, Jr. (Virginia, US)

Comfort

Read Jeremiah 29:1–14

'I know the plans I have for you,' declares the Lord, 'plans to prosper you and not to harm you, plans to give you hope and a future.'
Jeremiah 29:11 (NIV)

Today's quoted verse is one of the most popular scripture verses to memorise. And it should be. It's a lovely, encouraging verse. But a lot of people don't realise that this verse is part of a letter to exiles – the Israelites – who still have 70 years of captivity ahead of them. God isn't saying those words to happy, comfortable people in their comfortable homes with their comfortable families. God is speaking to people going through some tough stuff.

It's easy to take comfort in that verse without the context. But with the context, it is even more meaningful. I found that especially true in my case as I battled cancer. My cancer wasn't a punishment in the way that the Israelites' exile was, but it was the toughest season of my life. Some moments I was a little scared of what lay ahead for me, and some moments I was very scared. But in many moments I had more peace than a 40-year-old wife and mother with breast cancer should have.

That peace came from God, who has plans to prosper me and not to harm me. I'm so thankful that the same words that gave the Israelites comfort thousands of years ago can still be a comfort to us today.

Prayer: *Dear Lord, thank you for bringing us comfort in hard times. Help us to sense your presence, even when circumstances make it hard. Amen*

Thought for the day: No matter what my situation is, God speaks words of comfort to me.

Kim Harms (Iowa, US)

Every detail matters

Read Psalm 104:10–24

Many, Lord my God, are the wonders you have done, the things you planned for us. None can compare with you; were I to speak and tell of your deeds, they would be too many to declare.
Psalm 40:5 (NIV)

On a hot afternoon, I went to pick up my five-year-old from school. We had to walk because we couldn't afford the bus fare. I was in a hurry, sweating profusely and wishing I had a car.

On the way home, a hen crossed our path. With innocent amazement, my daughter asked, 'Mummy, why is the hen's thumb at the back of its leg?' I laughed before answering, 'Without the thumb, the hen wouldn't be able to balance itself well.'

I was slightly embarrassed as I answered her question. I realised that while I was dwelling on the difficulty of our current situation, my little girl was taking in the wonderful works of God's creation. For weeks, I had been so engrossed in our family's problems that I had failed to recognise and appreciate the little things. When I focused on God's perfect creation and the vital details God designed, I realised that every detail of my life matters to God as well.

Prayer: *Thank you, Lord, for caring for even the smallest details of our lives. Help us to remember that everything works together to bring glory and praise to you. Amen*

Thought for the day: God cares for every part of my life.

Catherine Kwao (Accra, Ghana)

A simple ministry

Read Matthew 25:31–40

The King will reply, 'Truly I tell you, whatever you did for one of the least of these brothers and sisters of mine, you did for me.'
Matthew 25:40 (NIV)

One day while we were waiting for the bus, my mother talked to a fellow passenger about his need for Christ. I noticed that he listened carefully and that her witness made an impression on him. My mother loved people and was always eager to share her faith.

When I was preparing for ministry I listened to lectures describing how to be a witness. But when I share my faith today, I remember Mum's witness for Jesus. Her desire to share Christ was based on a real concern for others, not an exercise based on a step-by-step method taught in a classroom.

Mum's actions impressed upon me that her faith was real and that she wanted everyone she met to know about Christ's saving power. My mother did not consider herself a minister. Yet she fed people, prayed with those who needed prayer and encouraged those who were discouraged. She simply did what needed to be done to help others and to share her faith.

I learned from my mother's example that sharing our faith doesn't have to be complicated or follow a particular method. It's something any of us can do every day – wherever we are.

Prayer: *Dear God, help us as we share your love and the story of salvation with others. In Jesus' name. Amen*

Thought for the day: Wherever we are today we can be a witness for Christ.

Thad H. Carter (Texas, US)

Sacred relationships

Read Romans 5:1–6

Bear one another's burdens, and in this way you will fulfil the law of Christ.
Galatians 6:2 (NRSV)

In 2014, I learned that I had a brain tumour. After five hours of surgery, the doctors found out that it was inoperable. Instead, I had to undergo radiation to shrink the tumour in an effort to prevent further damage and growth.

This was a devastating blow. I was 80, and I had lived a full, healthy and independent life. Now I was forced to make adjustments because of permanent damage to my eyesight, and to my pituitary, adrenal and other systems. I could no longer drive, which altered my formerly active lifestyle – especially in my church and community activities. But shortly after my return home from the radiation treatment, some women from my church volunteered to drive me anywhere I needed to go. They have done this for more than three years, and in the process we have become close friends, enriching one another's lives.

Through my struggle and the way my community has cared for me, God has taught me the valuable lesson from Galatians 6:2 about the need for interdependence in Christian community. Now I more fully appreciate the sacredness of relationships. I have realised that life is short and that I should make haste to love, be quick to show kindness and be eager to help others.

Prayer: *O God, help us to be open to your will for us in every circumstance of our lives. Amen*

Thought for the day: In any experience, God offers me opportunities to learn.

Luleen S. Anderson (North Carolina, US)

Max

Read John 10:1–14

[The gatekeeper] calls his own sheep by name and leads them out.
John 10:3 (NRSV)

My cat, Max, isn't very smart, but he is very affectionate and loves people. Every day at breakfast, he puts his paws on my leg for his morning head scratch. When I get up and go into the bathroom, he comes running upstairs and meows with panic because he can't see me anymore and doesn't know where I am. Then, every time, I open the door and call to him, 'It'll be okay, Max,' and he calms down.

Sometimes my relationship with God is like that. God is always there – close to me every day – but sometimes I lose focus and forget. When I lose my sense of his presence I feel disconnected and troubled. But if I cry out, he calls me by name and reassures me. Sometimes I don't feel very smart, but – out of an abundance of love and grace – God is always patient with me.

Prayer: *Dear God, by your grace, help us to listen for and follow your voice. As Jesus taught us, we pray, 'Our Father which art in heaven, Hallowed be thy name. Thy kingdom come, Thy will be done in earth, as it is in heaven. Give us this day our daily bread. And forgive us our debts, as we forgive our debtors. And lead us not into temptation, but deliver us from evil: For thine is the kingdom, and the power, and the glory, for ever. Amen.'**

Thought for the day: When I am lost, God calls me by name.

Raymond Lockley (California, US)

PRAYER FOCUS: THOSE FEELING SEPARATED FROM GOD
Matthew 6:9–13 (KJV)

Children know better

Read Matthew 18:1–5

Jesus [replied], 'Have you never read, "From the lips of children and infants you, Lord, have called forth your praise"?'
Matthew 21:16 (NIV)

One day as we were preparing for an outing, my four-year-old son said that we should pray before we left. When asked what he would like to pray for, he said, 'Let's thank God for Jesus.'

When we help our children to grow in their faith, they in turn can give us an entirely different perspective. I have prayed throughout my life, giving thanks for all the blessings that I receive on a daily basis. Sometimes too many of my blessings go unnoticed. But my son reminded me that we are surrounded by blessings every day. One of the greatest blessings we have received is Jesus, God's Son, through whom grace is made available to each of us. My four-year-old son reminded me of this fact that day.

No one knows the kingdom of God better than children. And that is why Jesus tells us to be like them in our faith.

Prayer: *Dear Lord, we thank you for Jesus and for the abundant grace that you have made available through him. Amen*

Thought for the day: Today I will thank God for the gift of grace through Jesus Christ.

Deepika Emmanuel Sagar (Rajasthan, India)

Peace in the storm

Read Psalm 46:1–3

If your Instruction hadn't been my delight, I would have died because of my suffering.
Psalm 119:92 (CEB)

For the first time in all the years I had lived in Florida, a hurricane threatened our home. I had seen the destruction that is created in the wake of a devastating storm, but never before had it been so personal. As we anxiously watched the reports of the pummelling of islands in its path, we prepared our home as best we could and sought safer ground on which to wait it out.

The waiting was filled with fear, uncertainty and stress. We had no way of knowing exactly where the storm would hit and what its aftermath would be. We worried not only for ourselves but for our friends and family. And we prayed.

Through it all, one constant brought me peace: I knew that God was with us and would see us through, no matter what the hurricane left in its wake. When the winds had died down and we began the trip home, I was at peace knowing that – no matter what awaited us – we would get through it with God by our side.

Prayer: *Heavenly Father, help us to remember that no storm in life is too devastating for you to handle. Amen*

Thought for the day: In every trial, I can lean on the Lord.

Trish Krider (Florida, US)

New purpose

Read 1 Samuel 3:1–10

In all things God works for the good of those who love him, who have been called according to his purpose.
Romans 8:28 (NIV)

Many years ago, a car accident resulted in the traumatic amputation of my left leg and compression fractures of five vertebrae in my back. I was in the army at the time and at the top of my pay grade, but this injury resulted in my medical retirement from the service. For many months in the hospital I questioned why God had allowed this to happen. I sometimes cursed him for the pain I was having and for taking me away from a job I loved. For many months I suffered from depression.

Then, while attending my secondary school reunion, I renewed my friendship with a classmate; and in a very short time we married. A former medical social worker, she applied to volunteer at a hospital and later volunteered me to perform magic tricks for children who were receiving treatment. In a short time this mission of performing expanded to three other hospitals, and for 18 years we brought smiles and joy to those children.

Soon after beginning our mission, parents whom we had seen in the paediatric wards began to thank us for bringing joy to their children. Only when we decided to retire from our hospital work did I fully realise how God had been at work, even in that traumatic time after my accident, to prepare me to bring happiness to others.

Prayer: *Dear God, help us to see the new purpose that you have built into every dead end we encounter. Amen*

Thought for the day: I can examine today's loss to find tomorrow's service for God.

John S. McClenahan (Nevada, US)

I choose you

Read 1 Timothy 1:12–16

Jesus said to [the Pharisees], 'It is not the healthy who need a doctor, but those who are ill. I have not come to call the righteous, but sinners.'
Mark 2:17 (NIV)

I was in the prison yard reading my Bible when another inmate approached me and began to tell me about some issues he was dealing with. I talked to him for about 20 minutes before I needed to leave to attend the service in the chapel. 'Can I come with you?' he asked. Without hesitating, I said yes. After the service concluded, he asked me to wait for him while he spoke to the chaplain. After they had talked for a while, they came over to me.

The chaplain said to me, 'I hear you know a thing or two about the Bible.' He went on to ask me if I would be interested in teaching a Bible study class. I tried to explain to him that I didn't think I could, and he asked me if it was because of something I had done in my past. I nodded. He said, 'God doesn't just use the ones who are ready; he gets ready the ones he wants to use.' I went on to teach the Bible study class.

From this, I learned the valuable lesson that God can use any of us, regardless of the circumstances of our lives.

Prayer: *Dear God, help us to bring others closer to you by ministering to them wherever we are. Amen*

Thought for the day: Regardless of my past, God can still use me.

K. Smith (Ohio, US)

The power of faith

Read Psalm 18:1–6

In my distress I called to the Lord; I cried to my God for help. From his temple he heard my voice; my cry came before him, into his ears.
Psalm 18:6 (NIV)

I was born into a Christian home and from a young age took part in the children's activities in my church. As an adult, I worked as a children's teacher and later as a counsellor for teenagers. Still, I never imagined the magnitude of the impact that God would have on my life.

It started one afternoon when my world collapsed. The doctor informed me that I had a large cyst on an ovary and needed surgery. The pains were becoming more and more intense and unbearable, and my fear and anguish increased daily. Every day I pleaded with God to have mercy on me and to remove that cyst from my body.

On the day of the next medical examination, I prayed, asking God for strength and courage to face and accept the final result. While I was being examined I observed the face of the doctor looking for the cyst. Puzzled, he said in a low voice, 'I cannot find anything; the cyst is not there.' When I heard that, my heart filled with joy. My heart was beating fast. I had no doubt that the power of God had manifested itself. I left the hospital glorifying God for the results. I am sure that we can trust in God because he is able to do all things.

Prayer: *Almighty God, thank you for listening to our prayers and sustaining us. Help us to accept the outcome of our struggles, knowing you are always with us. Amen*

Thought for the day: When I am attuned to God's power, I am amazed at what he can do.

Ruth R. Mancilla Casalez (Estado de Mexico, Mexico)

Lord, hold my hand

Read Romans 8:38–39

I am the Lord your God who takes hold of your right hand and says to you, Do not fear; I will help you.
Isaiah 41:13 (NIV)

'Hold my hand as we cross this road, son,' I said to my then-five-year-old. 'No, Mama. You hold my hand,' he responded. As we rushed across the road, I wondered about his request; so later I asked him what he meant when he asked me to hold his hand.

'Well, my hand is small and I might lose your hand, but your hand is stronger than mine. If you hold my hand I know you won't let go of me.' His trust in me warmed my heart.

We often have the idea that we must hang on to God with all our might lest we get separated from him and lose our way. I'm so glad to know that God promises to take hold of my hand, because his hand is much stronger than mine and I know that he will never let go of me.

I say along with Paul that nothing is able to separate us from the love of God; he is holding on to us, and nothing will ever come between his hand and ours.

Prayer: *Holy Father, on those days when we are afraid and feel all alone, help us to feel the warmth of your hand holding ours. Amen*

Thought for the day: My heavenly Father will never let go of my hand.

Dorcas Elizabeth Andrews (Alabama, US)

Stiles

Read Psalm 23

I will instruct you and teach you in the way you should go.
Psalm 32:8 (NIV)

On a country walk with friends we encountered a series of stiles, allowing access from field to field but keeping livestock secure. Some were vertical narrow gaps that allowed us through but were not wide enough for animals; others, built of stone or wood, were quite a challenge and even hazardous where the ground was muddy or uneven.

It occurred to me that stiles have many parallels with life's journey: for some they represent a barrier, and in the same way we come up against barriers that seem impossible to surmount. Stiles need maintenance, and we too need to keep fit physically and spiritually. At some stiles, a helping hand is invaluable; in the same way, life's problems can be eased by skilled professional guidance or the love and compassion of others.

Usually stiles are placed on well-defined pathways. If we stray from these paths, we may cause damage, injure ourselves, cause a farmer expense or threaten the safety of livestock. Similarly we can consider our journey through life, the pitfalls that may occur and the wisdom of being guided by our Lord and Saviour.

Prayer: *Lord, help us to keep on your pathway and guide us safely when we encounter obstacles on our path. Amen*

Thought for the day: How can I help others I meet on the pathway today?

Brian Beeson (Derbyshire, England)

Real-life good Samaritans

Read Luke 10:25–37

A Samaritan, as he travelled, came where the man was; and when he saw him, he took pity on him.

Luke 10:33 (NIV)

A good friend of mine was mugged one evening after getting off a bus in the city. Unfortunately, at first no one came to his aid. Then two young men arrived on the scene. They chased the mugger away, called an ambulance and then sat with my friend until it arrived. As they waited, my friend discovered that these two young men were immigrant Muslims. While no one else would stop to help, it was two strangers who showed him true kindness.

In Jesus' parable of the good Samaritan, the people who might have been expected to stop and help did not, while the unlikely candidate did. Perhaps we could all benefit from examining the way we view others. When we look through Jesus' eyes, we don't see their background or the colour of their skin; we see each person as Jesus sees them – made in the image of the creator.

Prayer: *Thank you, Lord, for using unlikely heroes to help those in need. Help us to see each person through your eyes and to value every person as your beloved creation. In Jesus' name. Amen*

Thought for the day: When I look through Jesus' eyes, I can see value in every person.

Tracy Krauss (British Columbia, Canada)

PRAYER FOCUS: THOSE WHO RISK THEIR SAFETY FOR OTHERS

God's special creation

Read Psalm 139:13–18

You created my inmost being; you knit me together in my mother's womb. I praise you because I am fearfully and wonderfully made.
Psalm 139:13–14 (NIV)

I struggled with depression and a poor sense of self-worth. 'Is life really worth living when I'll always be so mediocre?' I asked myself. I had been going to church only sporadically, but my mother insisted I start going regularly. Early on, I heard a sermon about how we were all created in God's image and are pleasing to him. Later in the week, I attended a small group where people talked openly about issues they were dealing with. When I shared my depression and feelings of worthlessness, I was surprised to discover that many people were dealing with the same issues.

God seemed to be speaking through me as I told them that I would always be there for any of them who needed me. Every week since then, I have been helping the people in the group. I think maybe I've discovered my special gift, which is helping others. Now I'm pursuing a doctorate in psychology. I've learned that – at just the right time – God will show each of us our particular gift of service.

Prayer: *Thank you, almighty God, for sending your Son to die for our sins and for creating us individually and uniquely. Help us to use wisely whatever gift you've given us. Amen*

Thought for the day: God designed me with special gifts to use in his service.

Kevin Alch (Texas, US)

'I've got you!'

Read Isaiah 41:1–10

Do not fear, for I am with you; do not be dismayed, for I am your God. I will strengthen you and help you; I will uphold you with my righteous right hand.
Isaiah 41:10 (NIV)

My first summer church ministry was to accompany a youth leader on a number of wilderness trips in the White Mountains of New Hampshire. Each adventure ended with a rock-climbing activity. I am not fond of heights but agreed to take part, thinking, 'How tall can a cliff be in New England?' But at the bottom of a 300-foot cliff, my fear kicked in. Our expert guide was secured at the top of the cliff and waited for his assistant to tie me into the harness. I slowly began my clumsy ascent. At 20 feet, I almost froze with fear, but I heard the voice of the guide above me: 'I've got you!' As long as I kept a tight hold on the rope, I felt sure that he was there and guiding me. His encouragement and instructions helped me to make the climb. By following his voice, I eventually made it to the top.

Jesus promised that he would always be with us and that he would uphold us through anything we might encounter. When we feel as if we are hanging off a tall cliff with no help in sight, we can recall the promises of God to be with us through it all. He will hold us tightly and instruct us in the way we should go. If we listen, we will hear the encouraging words of the Lord: 'I've got you!'

Prayer: *Wonderful Lord, thank you for reassuring us that you are greater than anything we may face. Amen*

Thought for the day: God is my ever-present help in times of trouble (see Psalm 46:1).

James Baumberger (Connecticut, US)

The way

Read John 14:1–7

Jesus said to [Thomas], 'I am the way, and the truth, and the life. No one comes to the Father except through me.'
John 14:6 (NRSV)

In the last few years, I have done a lot of travelling. I often don't give a second thought to exploring a new place without a proper guide. As a result, I am frequently uncertain if I have the correct address or if the directions I've been given are complete. At times, I have to search for street names where there aren't any. Or, at other times, the directions I've been given use points of reference that are unfamiliar to me.

While some of my travel situations can be frustrating, they remind me of what's important in my faith journey. I know that we are all travellers, but not all of us are going in the right direction. It is good to have, receive and give the directions that lead to eternal life. We can be confident in the directions we find through scripture because Jesus is clear that he is the way that leads to eternal life.

Prayer: *Merciful God, we ask you to continue to guide us on the path that leads to eternal life. In the name of Jesus who taught us to pray, saying, 'Our Father in heaven, hallowed be your name, your kingdom come, your will be done on earth as it is in heaven. Give us today our daily bread. Forgive us our debts, as we also have forgiven our debtors. And lead us not into temptation, but deliver us from the evil one.'* Amen*

Thought for the day: I can be confident in God's guidance.

Priscilla E. Chaves (Alajuela, Costa Rica)

*Matthew 6:9–13 (NIV)

Wherever I am

Read Isaiah 55:10–12

My word that goes out from my mouth… will not return to me empty, but will accomplish what I desire and achieve the purpose for which I sent it.
Isaiah 55:11 (NIV)

I had spent over ten years as a minister, and then one day I found myself without a church. Much of my identity had come from being a minister. What identity did I have as an unemployed one? With a daughter to feed, I needed a job quickly. Then, through a strange series of events, I received an offer to drive a taxi. Running out of options, I accepted.

I wasn't the most enthusiastic taxi driver – at least in the beginning. Perhaps I was arrogant and thought it beneath me. God wasn't going to let me get away with that, though.

One day I was driving a woman who had a drug addiction home from the hospital after her close call with death. We had a sincere conversation, and when she got out of the taxi she said, 'Thank you for that moment of peace and for listening.' Though brief, ours was a true connection. Later that evening I was blessed to see a spectacular sunset of golden pink hues from the taxi, and peace about my vocation washed over me. Suddenly I knew that God would use me for ministry no matter where I ended up – whether in a pulpit or a taxi.

Our God is so expansive that he was able to pitch a tent for the sun (see Psalm 19:4). Every day he gives us fresh revelations; we only have to pay attention. Thanks be to God!

Prayer: *Dear God, help us not to miss new insights about how to serve you. Amen*

Thought for the day: Ministry can happen anywhere.

Jessica Zolondek (US)

Our dwelling place

Read Psalm 27:1–14

The Lord is my light and my salvation – whom shall I fear? The Lord is the stronghold of my life – of whom shall I be afraid?
Psalm 27:1 (NIV)

When our girls were young, the older ones would play 'I'm going to get you' with whoever was the youngest at the time. Invariably, the youngest would run to me or her mother and attempt to hide behind our legs. She knew that she was safe as long as we were around.

This reminds me of the way that King David knew he was safe as long as he remained in the presence of God. Today's reading shows David's total reliance upon God when he called the Lord his light, salvation and stronghold and expressed his longing to remain in the house of the Lord all the days of his life. He was not talking about bricks and mortar. God was David's dwelling place. Living daily in the presence of the Lord brought David comfort and gave him confidence over his enemies.

As I meditated on this psalm, a sobering question pushed its way to the front of my thinking. When do I run to the Lord? Is it only when I am already afraid? Is it only when I have a need? My honest answers humbled me. I often seek God in times of want or times of fear, but when things are going well I sometimes forget to feel delight that he is always with me. Like my girls are with me, I am happy to know that God is my hiding place in times of trouble. But like David, we can be overjoyed that God is our dwelling place.

Prayer: *Dear Lord, help us to bask in your presence at all times. Amen*

Thought for the day: God's constant presence gives me confidence to overcome my fears.

Alonza Jones (Alabama, US)

A grandfather's love

Read Ephesians 1:3–14

As a prisoner for the Lord… I urge you to live a life worthy of the calling you have received.
Ephesians 4:1 (NIV)

I cannot imagine the intense grief my biological grandfather must have felt when my new adoptive family picked me up. He knew that it would be the last time he would see me. At just six years old, I was 'Grandpa's girl', the one he would balance on his hands, the one who would grab his big cowboy hat and put it on her own head. Giving me up for adoption broke my grandfather's heart. But out of his great love for me, he wanted something better for my life than what he could provide.

When I think of everything that my grandfather gave up for me, I remember God's heart-wrenching sacrifice in offering up Jesus. Like my grandfather, God wanted something better for us, a life not separated from him because of sin. So God sacrificed his only Son as an atonement for our sins so we could be adopted and become heirs to his kingdom.

Every day, I am determined to live a life that my grandfather would be proud of. Even more so, when I think what God, through Jesus, did for me, I am humbled to live a life worthy of my calling.

Prayer: *Loving Father, thank you for adopting us as your children. Give us the courage to confess our sins and release them to you. Amen*

Thought for the day: I want to live a life worthy of God's great love and sacrifice.

Anne Hayton (Indiana, US)

Never forsaken

Read Deuteronomy 31:5–8

Yea, though I walk through the valley of the shadow of death, I will fear no evil: for thou art with me.
Psalm 23:4 (KJV)

A couple of years ago, I was diagnosed with an enlarged prostate. This stressful time was followed by a series of hospital visits, examinations and tests. Daily, my family and I prayed and trusted in God to heal me. When further tests revealed prostate cancer, my family was devastated. However, throughout surgery to remove the cancerous cells – with its attendant side effects, health challenges and physical limitations – we had a sense of confidence that all would be well. Along with the psalmist, I could say, 'Yea, though I walk through the valley of the shadow of death, I will fear no evil: for thou art with me.'

In our reading for today, Joshua must have felt such a sense of anxiety and trouble in being appointed to lead God's people into the promised land that he needed firm assurance from God through Moses: 'Do not be afraid or terrified because of them, for the Lord your God goes with you; he will never leave you nor forsake you' (Deuteronomy 31:6, NIV).

As God's children, we all abide in this assurance. Though our situations and circumstances may be difficult or our health may fail, God is present to go through it with us. One year later, I could once again testify with the psalmist: 'Good and upright is the Lord' (Psalm 25:8, NIV).

Prayer: *Thank you, Lord, for your comfort and healing power over us all. In Jesus' name, we pray. Amen*

Thought for the day: God is faithful in all circumstances.

Mike Anwana (Ad Dawhah, Qatar)

'Are you the one?'

Read Matthew 11:1–6

[Jesus said,] 'Blessed is anyone who takes no offence at me.'
Matthew 11:6 (NRSV)

In today's reading, we find that John the Baptist was imprisoned because of his preaching. While he was in prison, John heard about the works of Jesus and sent two of his disciples to ask, 'Are you the one who is to come, or should we expect someone else?' (NIV). John's question puzzled me. Hadn't John preached about Jesus and even baptised him? (See Matthew 3:11–17.) Was John hoping that Jesus would come and rescue him?

Like John, as a follower of Christ, I sometimes have doubts. Even though I know in my heart that God is real and trustworthy, at times I still wrestle with questions like, 'Lord, are you there? Do you really care that I'm going through these difficulties?' I recall once praying earnestly, but the answer I sought did not come. I felt as if God had let me down. I was upset and bewildered, and asked, 'Why, Lord?' After calming down, I felt as if God was asking me, 'Do you still love me? Do you still believe in me?'

I can remember and identify with Jesus' reply to John's question, 'Blessed is anyone who takes no offence at me.' Even when I don't understand why the answers to my prayers are slow in coming or come in different ways from what I expected, I still believe that God is faithful and loves me.

Prayer: *Dear Lord, when disappointments come our way, please help our faith and love for you to remain strong. Amen*

Thought for the day: Even when my prayers seem unanswered, God still loves me.

Victoria P. Creel (Alabama, US)

Eternal love

Read 2 Corinthians 5:1–10

We who are still alive and are left will be caught up together with them in the clouds to meet the Lord in the air. And so we will be with the Lord for ever. Therefore encourage one another with these words.
1 Thessalonians 4:17–18 (NIV)

My son Ted died in a car crash in March 1978. It has been a long time, and though some people say you get over it, you don't; you just learn to live with it. I remember the night he died I said to my wife, 'I want to know where he's gone.' I went in search, and that journey led me to church, to theological college and eventually to full-time ministry. I learned that my son had come into the presence of the Lord. My son had faith in Jesus Christ, who loved him so much that he died on a cross some 2,000 years ago. Because of his faith, Ted is in the presence of the Lord, full of vigour and happiness.

You never get over the death of anyone you love as much as I love my son, and you don't want to. That is the kind of love that is in our hearts and in God's heart when Jesus said: 'That day you will know that I am in my Father, and you in me, and I in you' (John 14:20, NRSV). I miss my son, but I am at peace because he is in the presence of God.

Prayer: *Dear God, help us to know that we can never be separated from your love because of our Lord Jesus Christ. Amen*

Thought for the day: How can I inspire others to seek a relationship with God?

Jon C. Goeringer (Maryland, US)

Amazing world

Read Psalm 147:1–11

[The Lord] covers the heavens with clouds, prepares rain for the earth, makes grass grow on the hills.
Psalm 147:8 (NRSV)

I'm fascinated by the wonders of the natural world: the delicate structure of a leaf, a rainstorm with loud claps of thunder and flashes of lightning, the way thousands of ants march in single file across the garden to an unknown destination. I enjoy listening to the myriad sounds made by a variety of birds and insects: humming, chirping, squeaking, twittering and singing melodiously to one another. When I pause for a moment to notice all of the life around me, I am awed by God's creative powers.

One afternoon, years ago, I looked up at the sky and saw a spectrum – part of a rainbow, visible on a cloud – and I pointed it out to my friend. I'd never seen such a phenomenon before. He said, 'I'm sure God can do better than that.'

I felt hurt by his comment. Of course, God can do great things, but the little things are also demonstrations of his presence, love and wisdom. I thank God for the many ways – large and small – in which his presence is revealed in my life and in the world.

Prayer: *Thank you, God, for this amazing world that you have created. Help us to recognise all the ways you are present with us. In Jesus' name. Amen*

Thought for the day: God is present all around me.

Sister Confianza del Señor (Colón, Honduras)

Cover to cover

Read 2 Timothy 3:14–17

All scripture is inspired by God and is useful for teaching, for reproof, for correction, and for training in righteousness.
2 Timothy 3:16 (NRSV)

Nearly 20 years ago, I decided to read the Bible from beginning to end. I'm pleased to say that I did it; I'm not pleased to say that it usually felt like a chore and that often I was distracted when reading it. My desire to know scripture more deeply had backfired as I found myself wishing I could read some previous passages that had spoken to me rather than the three chapters I had assigned myself for the day.

Ultimately, I learned an important lesson. God's word does not always have to be approached in a particular order or in a systematic fashion. Rather, scripture comes to our minds in all sorts of unique ways and times. For everything there is a season, and I've grown to feel that way about Bible passages: some verses that speak to me now may not speak to me in the same way much later in life. In turn, others may mean little to me until suddenly they profoundly impact my current situation.

God is revealed to us every day. We need not impose an order to those revelations. Through prayer, devotion and other forms of worship, we each walk a Christian path that may not follow a direct line from Genesis to Revelation.

Prayer: *Dear God, thank you for revealing yourself to us in unique ways that help us on our Christian paths. Amen*

Thought for the day: In which scripture verse can I find new meaning today?

Andrew Billings (Alabama, US)

Seeking guidance

Read Proverbs 3:5–12
In all your ways acknowledge [the Lord], and he will make straight your paths.
Proverbs 3:6 (NRSV)

Throughout my life I have faced situations where I was uncertain of what to do and was afraid of making choices on my own. Before I truly entrusted my life to God, I believed that every aspect of my life had a 50% chance of success; if I made the wrong choice, I would fail. Unfortunately, I often doubted my decisions and would spend hours regretting the things I did.

After a few years, I grew to understand Christ's power and faithfulness more clearly. My problems became less stressful and I began to rely fully on the Lord to guide me, trusting that God would lead me to good things.

I regularly remind myself of the motto 'God is good all the time.' It is easy to forget it during times of distress. When we remember that God is always by our side, we can stop focusing on smaller issues and find great comfort. When we seek God's will, we can live in confidence knowing that he is always working for good.

Prayer: *Dear Lord, we thank you for the lives you have given us. Help us find comfort in you and trust that you are guiding us towards the good. Amen*

Thought for the day: Because God is faithful, I can live confidently.

Ed Romero (Texas, US)

An hour well spent

Read Isaiah 46:3–9

[The Lord says,] 'I am he who will sustain you.'
Isaiah 46:4 (NIV)

One of the most vivid memories from my childhood is seeing my mother retreat to the living room each day at three o'clock for an hour of prayer. This was her special time, and we knew not to interrupt her unless it was something important. Even after I left home, if I called my parents in the afternoon, Dad would gently remind me that it was Mum's prayer time.

This kind of sacred time revealed her loving, trusting relationship with God. Mum spent that hour with her best friend, not only sharing what was on her mind but spending quiet time listening with her heart.

Many years have passed, and now my mum lives in a nursing home. She is no longer able to pray as she once did, but I am confident that her relationship with God is as strong as ever. I see in her peacefulness and acceptance that I believe is the fruit of her many years of prayer.

My mum is a living reminder of God's promise, clearly spoken by the prophet Isaiah. I am certain that God will never abandon my mum – or any of us.

Prayer: *O God, help us to remember to set apart time each day to spend with you in prayer. Amen*

Thought for the day: Time spent with God in prayer is never wasted.

Andrea Woronick (Connecticut, US)

PRAYER FOCUS: MOTHERS IN NURSING HOMES

The courage-giving father

Read Joshua 1:1–9

Be strong and courageous. Do not be afraid; do not be discouraged, for the Lord your God will be with you wherever you go.
Joshua 1:9 (NIV)

When I was seven years old, my younger brother and I were playing near our family's clothing shop. Then the local bully came up to us and started slapping me and hitting me on the head. I was terrified. I ran to my parents, but the shop was full of customers and they sent me away. Humiliated and in pain, I sat in a corner and cried.

That evening my dad noticed that I was still upset and he asked me what was wrong. I told him what had happened. My father comforted me and told me that if the bully came near me again, I had to face him with courage and warn him that my father would come to my aid if I asked. My fears left me, and I felt I had received the strength of a lion. I waited for the bully the next evening. When I stood my ground and warned him about my father, the bully ran away.

I am now a father myself and my children come to me for help. When I meet adversity, I find courage in my heavenly Father. God promises always to be with us and to protect us. These promises give us strength in knowing that we can turn to our heavenly Father for courage and comfort.

Prayer: *Heavenly Father, thank you for being by our side and comforting us when we face adversity. Lead us with courage and divine strength. Amen*

Thought for the day: With God, I can face challenges with courage.

David Livingstone (Bangalore, India)

Play days

Read Mark 6:30–32

In returning and rest you shall be saved; in quietness and in trust shall be your strength.
Isaiah 30:15 (NRSV)

I wonder why I'm so busy. Has life always been this frantic? I'm thankful for my study where I can think, write and spend time with God. Unfortunately, it's not proof against interruptions and phone calls! Not far away, however, is an Anglican convent where you can book a room when you need some peace and quiet. It's welcoming, steeped in prayer, with an almost tangible stillness. Here I can 'do my own thing' before God: meditating, drawing or reading. These are my 'play days'. I may arrive tired or frustrated, head full of chaotic thoughts, carrying the weight of the world. I drop my mess at God's feet and wait. God's okay with this. I don't have to prove anything – just allow his healing peace to seep deep into my heart.

Perhaps this is what happened when Jesus and his disciples took a slow boat ride across the Sea of Galilee, suspended on the waves between one clamouring crowd and the next. It gave them pause to chat, snooze and ponder.

Time out is so important for our mental and spiritual well-being. At the end of my 'play day', though, it's back to reality. I stuff my papers and pens in my bag and head for home, re-energised and eager to share the treasures of my day.

Prayer: *Loving God, we pray for all who feel stressed and weary. Help them to find rest and renewal in you. Amen*

Thought for the day: How can I take time out to be with God?

April McIntyre (Derbyshire, England)

Running aground

Read Acts 27:21–26
Keep up your courage… for I have faith in God that it will be exactly as I have been told. But we will have to run aground on some island.
Acts 27:25–26 (NRSV)

On my first day of a new job, I found myself sitting in the office feeling terrified. For 13 years I had enjoyed working in a comfortable youth-ministry job for a couple of churches. During that time, I felt God calling me into something else but didn't really know what. I was interviewed for an insurance agency job and found myself in a new field, and the thought of all the contingencies and what-ifs made me fearful.

As I was trying to keep my head above water during the first few weeks in the job, God reminded me of the story about Paul's voyage to Rome. During Paul's trip a violent storm pummelled the vessel for a number of days, causing the crew to throw cargo off the ship and eventually leaving them without food. I imagine that the whole ordeal led them through the gamut of emotions, ending with the acceptance of imminent death. That's what panic can do. The wind and waves of our difficult situations often lead us to the logical conclusion that the end is near and God is absent.

Paul comforted and reassured the crew, stating that he had faith in what God had told him. In the midst of our storms we too can have courage that even when our lives 'run aground', God is still with us.

Prayer: *Dear Father, when we experience challenges, thank you for reassuring us of your care. Amen*

Thought for the day: Today I will trust that God is with me.

Robbie Mackenzie (Tennessee, US)

Letter for God

Read Psalm 28:6–9

Praise be to the Lord, for he has heard my cry for mercy.
Psalm 28:6 (NIV)

I can't remember the exact date when my sister made a paper bag and named it 'God's Bag', but it is still hanging in our bedroom. She said, 'If you ask something of God, you can write your request on a piece of paper, fold it and put it into God's Bag.'

Even though her method made me laugh, I realised that I also have a unique way of relating to God. Once, when I was particularly sad, I wrote all my feelings on a piece of paper and named it 'Letter for God'. In that letter, I told God all my requests. I didn't put it into God's Bag but saved it in my drawer under my clothes. A few months later, when I opened the letter, I smiled. The situation that had made me so sad was no more. Also, some of my requests had been fulfilled. In fact, I found that God had replaced my unfulfilled requests with something better.

Regardless of how we pray, God hears us. In Psalm 28:6, David says that God heard him when he called. God will do the same for us. We just have to remember to call.

Prayer: *Thank you, Lord, for always hearing us. We know that nothing can separate us from your love. Sustain us as we put our trust in you. Amen*

Thought for the day: No matter how I pray, God is listening.

Linawati Santoso (East Java, Indonesia)

PRAYER FOCUS: SOMEONE LEARNING TO PRAY

What a change!

Read 1 Corinthians 15:42–49

[The body is] weak when it's put into the ground, but it's raised in power.
1 Corinthians 15:43 (CEB)

I live and garden in the desert all year round. Among the things I grow are sugar snap peas. From the time I plant them, the peas will thrive for eight months and produce for more than five months. The plants climb on trellises to a height of more than eight feet. Sometimes it's hard to believe that such an abundant plant can grow from a small, wrinkled pea seed. But I have been planting pea seeds for years, so I can see the future plant in that seed. If I can see that kind of future in a pea seed, what does that mean when I have trusted Christ as my resurrection and my life?

The astonishing growth that God has hidden within my peas gives me great confidence that I will have even greater life eternally with God. When I look at a wrinkled pea, it reminds me of how I often feel. But then I find joy in knowing the kind of transformation a pea goes through before and after it is sown. Before I plant my peas, I soak them in water overnight; by morning they look brand new! Likewise, my body will be raised through the power of Jesus' resurrected life. When I meditate on the marvellous transformation of those wrinkled peas, I am overwhelmed with the thought of eternal life with Christ.

Prayer: *Creator God, thank you for the transformation hidden in a seed and for the wonder of what that transformation means to us – new life with you. Amen*

Thought for the day: No matter how small or wrinkled I feel, God can transform my life.

Mark Weinrich (Nevada, US)

Strengthen our hands

Read Nehemiah 6:1–15

All of them were trying to make us afraid, saying, 'They will be discouraged, and the work won't get finished.' But now, God, strengthen me!
Nehemiah 6:9 (CEB)

In December 2003 I was a mission worker in Liberia during the United Nations' disarmament process following a 14-year civil war. Upset and fearful, the child soldiers were refusing to turn in their arms.

At the theological college where I worked, gunshots from AK-47s could be heard right outside our office windows. Throughout the day my staff would jump under the tables at each sound of gunfire that seemed never to stop.

I began to pray as Nehemiah did. He refused to give in to the fear that was causing discouragement. Nehemiah shifted his focus away from those who were trying to frighten him and towards God. When we pray, God answers, and he gave Nehemiah spiritual discernment.

Fear is humanity's most deadly enemy. It can enslave us. During that time in Liberia, the Lord strengthened our minds, spirits and hands to continue the work of sharing the gospel. On any day we can follow Nehemiah's example and dispel fear by turning our thoughts and confidence to God.

Prayer: *God of all strength, when we are afraid, help us to trust you and to know that you will help us to complete any task you give us. Amen*

Thought for the day: Even in the gravest situations, God will give me courage.

Hattie L. Carlis (Indiana, US)

Never alone

Read Psalm 1:1–6

Keep straight the path of your feet, and all your ways will be sure.
Proverbs 4:26 (NRSV)

In my last year at school, I played sports, had friends and a girlfriend, and had good exam results. However, towards the end of the school year, my friends began behaving in ways that made me uncomfortable. Because of their new interests, I began spending less time with them. I went straight home after school and stopped seeing them at weekends. Even though they had been my closest friends, I had no desire to join them. I was hurt by the loss of my friendships and until the end of that year my days were lonely. I went to school and to sports practice, studied and slept.

I had gone to church my whole life, but I had never yearned to know God more than I did during those that year; he was revealed to me more each day. In the evenings, I loved going to church events where I learned about God and made new friends. I stopped hating my old friends and began praying for them.

In that year, God showed me that I was never alone. I didn't have to conform to the world to find community; I just needed to open my eyes and surrender to him.

Prayer: *Dear God, we thank you for your mercy, love and understanding. Thank you for comforting us in every circumstance. Amen*

Thought for the day: Today I will pray for an old friend.

Peyton Sherlin (Texas, US)

Expressions of love

Read 1 John 4:7–19

[Jesus said,] 'I give you a new commandment, that you love one another. Just as I have loved you, you also should love one another.'
John 13:34 (NRSV)

Each morning one of my colleagues goes to each office or section and greets each person with a smile and asks, 'How are you? How are things going with you?' If someone is absent, he inquires about them. I consider this friendly habit an expression of love. Our fast-paced, anxious society can minimise the importance of expressing love in our relationships with each other. It can be easy to forget the impact of simple actions like a warm greeting or a smile expressing care for someone.

As Christians, we are called to live by the fruit of the Spirit and to love one another. Jesus modelled the love we should show each other in practical, simple and daily ways: he shared meals with the disciples and with people on the margins of society and addressed the needs of women and lepers when no one else would. Jesus then showed us the ultimate expression of love by dying on the cross. Imitating such an example is a challenge, but even small actions can make a difference.

Prayer: *God of everlasting love, thank you for loving us completely. Teach us to love others like Jesus did. Amen*

Thought for the day: I follow Jesus' example when I love others.

Julianis Báez de Pichardo (Dominican Republic)

A constant companion

Read Psalm 73:23–28
Come near to God and he will come near to you.
James 4:8 (NIV)

Recently, one of my students and I were alone outside. Out of the blue, he asked me, 'Why do I have to believe in God?' I answered, 'Well, you don't have to believe in God; but I believe in him. I can't imagine my life without God.' We had a short discussion about God's care for his world, before moving on to another subject.

My student's question challenged me to think about why I believe in God. As I told my student, I can't imagine my life without my solid relationship with our creator. God is my constant companion, my Saviour and my best friend. I can talk to him about anything and everything. Early in the morning silence, I spend time alone with him as I drink my coffee. I tell him what's on my mind and ask for guidance.

Throughout the day I pray, 'Help me, Lord!' or 'Please, Lord' or 'What do you think, Lord?' Lately I find myself offering confession at bedtime and saying, 'I'm sorry, Lord.' It is comforting to know that God loves me, hears me, answers me and forgives me.

Prayer: *Thank you, God, for being a constant presence in our lives. We need you in all the circumstances of our day-by-day living. Amen*

Thought for the day: God stays close to me, and I will stay close to him.

Beth DeLong (Hawaii, US)

What really matters

Read Luke 6:47–49

Strive first for the kingdom of God and his righteousness, and all these things will be given to you as well.
Matthew 6:33 (NRSV)

My 92-year-old uncle lives by himself in Sarasota, Florida. As Hurricane Irma was about to hit southern Florida, he really didn't want to leave his house, but his children convinced him that it was time to go. He packed everything that meant something to him in two suitcases and left.

How simple things become during a storm! When it came to choosing what to take, 92 years of my uncle's life fit into two suitcases. News coverage is full of stories of people who prepared for, evacuated from and returned after record hurricane events. Some quotes we hear are 'Our house can be replaced, but our family can't' and 'The damage is awful, but we're so glad everyone is okay.' Repeatedly during storms we see that material things lose their importance, and things that really matter come to the forefront.

In today's scripture passage, we see that both men go through a storm. Their outcomes are different only because their foundations are different. This parable illustrates that the Christian life isn't about escaping the storms that come our way but about being able to weather the storms because of our foundation in Jesus Christ.

Prayer: *Dear God, as we weather life's storms, help us to build our lives on the firm foundation of your Son so that the world can see the source of our strength. Amen*

Thought for the day: During life's storms, Jesus is my foundation.

Dennis Denby (Illinois, US)

Still useful to God

Read Psalm 92:12–15
[The righteous] will still bear fruit in old age.
Psalm 92:14 (NIV)

As one of her contributions to our family, my grandmother would rip up old clothes into strips, sew the strips together and roll them into balls. She then used a large wooden hook to crochet the rags into colourful rugs. They were sometimes long, like a hall runner, and sometimes small to place beside a bed. When we got out of bed in the mornings, it was a comfort not to feel the cold floor of an unheated bedroom but instead to set our feet on to a soft rug. Those old clothes were no longer good for their original purpose but were now useful in a different way.

As we grow older, we may sometimes feel that we have outlived our usefulness. But God always has a purpose for our lives. We may not be able to do tasks that were easy for us when we were younger, but along the way we have gained knowledge and insight that we can share with others. Even into our senior years we can seek new ways to glorify God and serve others.

Prayer: *Gracious God, help us not to focus on what we cannot do but instead on what we can do to be useful in your service. Amen*

Thought for the day: With God's help I can bear fruit in any stage of life.

Mary Louise Stetser (New Jersey, US)

God's mysterious ways

Read Isaiah 40:28–31

Blessed is the one who trusts in the Lord, whose confidence is in him.
Jeremiah 17:7 (NIV)

When I started off on my morning walk, it was a bright and sunny day with no hint of rain. I walked through the hills and valleys, enjoying the beauty around me – the wind whipping up a wonderful dance of leaves and the crescendo of crickets chirping. Then, without warning, the weather changed, bringing a heavy rush of showers. Disappointed that the rain had disrupted my walk, I ran to take shelter in a small building by the wayside. As the rain continued, an elderly man joined me to escape the rain. We began to talk about the town where we lived. He had lived in the town for a long time, and he recounted many interesting stories of how it had changed over the years. When the rain stopped, we parted. While walking home I realised that just as the rain had come unannounced, new perspectives about life can arrive in unexpected ways.

Life is unpredictable, bringing difficulties to each of us. At first problems seem a burden, and we might want to curse our circumstances or blame God. Sometimes roadblocks lead to small miracles – or at least insights – that can shape our understanding, helping us to know God in a new way and to trust him more fully.

Prayer: *Dear Lord, help us to see that hindrances to our plans can bring us closer to you. Amen*

Thought for the day: Unexpected encounters can give me insights from God.

Palakunnathu A. Mathew (Kerala, India)

Redeeming love

Read 1 Corinthians 1:18–31
Let the one who boasts, boast in the Lord.
1 Corinthians 1:31 (NRSV)

In 2003, I was sent to hospital to receive treatment for my depression. My image as a minister's wife who had it all together was shattered. I spent two weeks alongside drug addicts, schizophrenics and alcoholics. By society's standards, we were failures and outcasts: weak, broken and ashamed.

As we each shared our stories, I watched the others give comfort and encouragement. They offered kind words, a touch or silent acceptance of 'you're not alone' and 'me too'. No one gave advice; no one condemned; no one judged or acted better than anyone else. After all, as hospital patients we could not pretend that we were well.

Romans 3:23–24 tells us that no distinctions exist among us since all 'fall short of the glory of God… [but] are now justified by [God's] grace as a gift'.

In today's reading, Paul reminded the Corinthian church that value does not lie in worldly wisdom, wealth or power; rather, it is our identity in Christ. In our weaknesses, Christ unites us and gives us his wisdom, wealth and power.

I no longer need to depend on my image as a pastor's wife for acceptance. Instead, in my brokenness, I reveal Christ and will boast in him.

Prayer: *Redeeming God, forgive us for wanting to look good before others. Remind us that it's only in you that we are made whole. Amen*

Thought for the day: God loves and accepts me as I am.

Jodi Harris (California, US)

Heart of gratitude

Read Mark 10:13–16

[Jesus said,] 'Let the little children come to me, and do not hinder them, for the kingdom of God belongs to such as these.'
Mark 10:14 (NIV)

My son has a severe form of dyslexia that makes schoolwork very difficult for him. I recently met with his teacher to design an education plan specifically for him.

After our long meeting, the teacher told me that my son comes to her at the end of each school day and thanks her for teaching him. I was deeply moved. I had no idea he did that! I know how much he dislikes school because it is so difficult for him. Yet he shows gratitude to his teacher in her efforts to help him.

I decided that I would do well to follow my son's example and try always to have such an attitude of gratitude, especially when it comes to my relationship with God. In today's passage from Mark's gospel, Jesus directs us to follow the example of a child. Even though some days are not pleasant or easy, having a heart of gratitude towards God reaps a heavenly reward.

Prayer: *Thank you, God, for all that you do and have done for us. Give us hearts of gratitude, purity and humility. In the name of Jesus, we pray. Amen*

Thought for the day: Beginning today I will more readily give thanks to God.

Karen Woodard (North Carolina, US)

God's wonderful word

Read John 1:1–5

Blessed is the one who reads aloud the words of the prophecy, and blessed are those who hear and who keep what is written in it.
Revelation 1:3 (NRSV)

I bought an electronic tablet to gain access to my emails. However, I quickly found out that the tablet contains many more applications. Soon I was exploring my new device in detail and deriving great pleasure from it.

In many ways, my response to the Bible is similar. My parents gave me my first Bible. When I was a boy in Sunday school, our teacher would announce a passage, and we would look it up. Sometimes we were asked to memorise a particular verse, which required me to look up the verse in my Bible at home. As the years passed and I began to read parts of the Bible on my own, I became more interested and – in the fullness of time – I gave my life to Christ.

That was only the beginning. The more I read the Bible, the more I wanted to read it. Later, as a Sunday school teacher and Bible class leader, I shared my knowledge of scripture with others. Although I no longer teach the Bible, I still read it on my own or with a study group. In addition, I refer to the Bible for guidance and often read it for relaxation. The more I explore God's word, the more I derive pleasure from it.

Prayer: *Dear Father, lead us day by day through your word. Amen*

Thought for the day: God's word can be my constant companion.

William Findlay (Scotland, United Kingdom)

Child of God

Read Luke 5:12–16

Live in harmony with one another. Do not be proud, but be willing to associate with people of low position. Do not be conceited.
Romans 12:16 (NIV)

My husband and I make it a practice to give physical goods rather than cash to someone in need. So when Jack asked me to hand money to the shivering woman on the pavement, I sensed the Holy Spirit was behind his request. I opened the car door, handed the money to the woman, and talked with her about her situation. Then I took her hands and prayed with her. After we had prayed, she wrapped me in a bear hug.

In that moment of touch I realised she was more than a shivering body behind a cardboard placard. Jesus touched those who were blind, suffering from leprosy or crippled, proclaiming that they were human beings worthy of concern and respect. The way they were regarded by their society did not minimise their worth.

I don't know what happened to her after that day, but I was forever changed by my encounter with that woman. I understood in a new way that I am no more deserving of God's healing touch than anyone else. We are equal in the eyes of God, who knows all and cares for all.

Prayer: *Open our eyes, O God, to see the needs around us and to hear the human hearts in need of your love. Amen*

Thought for the day: Today I will reach out to a struggling child of God.

Karen Wingate (Illinois, US)

Always in the stands

Read Psalm 68:4–10

*A father to the fatherless, a defender of widows, is God in his
holy dwelling.*
Psalm 68:5 (NIV)

When I was at school my father attended all of my activities – football games, basketball games, athletics tournaments. For a long time I thought it was only because of our close relationship. However, his support of student athletes continued until he was well into his 60s. Only at my father's funeral did I learn from my brother the true reason our father spent so much time at these events. My father had told him: 'When I was at school, my parents never came to anything because they were always drunk or at the pub. I go to all these activities for the kids whose parents don't turn up. They can count on me to be in the stands. I am always there so they have support from someone.'

Though my father wasn't religious, his example reminds me of the way our Lord shows us love and hope by never leaving us alone. Much as my father was always in the stands for the youngsters, when Jesus ascended into heaven, he left the Holy Spirit to comfort us. We can place total faith and hope in that truth.

Prayer: *Dear Father, continue to show us through others that you are always watching over us and guiding us along life's path. Amen*

Thought for the day: Like the best earthly fathers, God is always there for me.

Jason Robinson (Wisconsin, US)

The power of prayer

Read Ephesians 3:14–21

Whatever you ask for in prayer, believe that you have received it, and it will be yours.
Mark 11:24 (NIV)

I was born into a Christian family and we attended church every Sunday. But when my parents separated during my adolescence, I went through a crisis of faith. For many years, I asked: 'Does God exist? Why does God allow such suffering in my family?' I concentrated on my studies, continued my education and became a nurse. Then I got a job in a children's hospital.

I was one of the nurses on call in the emergency unit when a twelve-year-old girl named Alejandra was brought in. She was in a coma suffering from meningitis. The other nurse told me, 'Stay with Alejandra. I will manage the other patients in the unit.' I don't know why, but I started to pray. I prayed with faith throughout the night, trusting that the child would not die, that God would intercede. At 5.45 the next morning, just before my shift ended, Alejandra opened her eyes, took my hand and said, 'Beatriz.'

After this experience, I have maintained the discipline of prayer because I now understand that God is with us every moment and in every situation. He never abandons us.

Prayer: *Giver of all good things, you have plans for each of us. You know when our faith is vulnerable, and you respond to renew our hope. We thank you in Jesus' name. Amen*

Thought for the day: For whom will I pray today?

Beatriz Nasso (Uruguay)

Focus

Read Genesis 1:1–5

The heavens declare the glory of God; the skies proclaim the work of his hands.
Psalm 19:1 (NIV)

On 21 August 2017, people across the United States from Oregon to South Carolina were able to witness and experience a total solar eclipse, when the moon passed between the earth and the sun, blocking the sun's rays for several minutes. It was an amazing event that brought many people together around the world.

As I watched others gazing at this celestial sight, wearing protective solar glasses, I realised we were all focused on something much greater than ourselves. It also occurred to me that all our differences and opposing points of view had been laid aside; all our problems and concerns had been temporarily forgotten. We were united and joyful as we watched this stellar wonder of creation together.

I wonder what our lives and this world might look like if we tried to keep our hearts and minds just as focused on the wonderful, loving creator of the universe.

Prayer: *Heavenly Father, thank you for the wonders of creation. Help us to remain focused on you so that we can reflect your light and love in all that we say and do. Amen*

Thought for the day: Is my life focused on God?

Laura Andrews (Tennessee, US)

God's care

Read Matthew 7:7–11

God will fully satisfy every need of yours according to his riches in glory in Christ Jesus.
Philippians 4:19 (NRSV)

I grew up in the late 1930s, and my family was poor. Each evening we would sit down at the table, and Dad would read scripture to us five children and talk a little bit about what it meant. Then Mum would lead us in singing an old hymn before Dad said a prayer of thanks and blessed the food. But on many evenings, after Mum and Dad read scripture, sang and prayed, we would get up and leave the table because Mum had no food to prepare our evening meal. At those times, Dad would always say, 'Don't worry; God will see to it that we do not starve.' The next morning we would get up to find several baskets and sacks of food at the back door. None of us knew where they came from, but we did come to trust that the words in the scripture verse above were true.

I was only four when all this was happening, but I still remember those times of need and what God did for us. I am a witness that when we trusted and prayed, asking for help, God took care of us. Philippians 4:6 encourages us not to worry about anything, but to pray about everything.

Prayer: *Father God, thank you for being so loving and caring. Watch over all the people in the world who are hungry today. Amen*

Thought for the day: God's power is strongest when I am at my weakest (see 2 Corinthians 12:9–10).

John Cramer (Oklahoma, US)

Back to safety

Read Ezekiel 34:11–15

Thus says the Lord God: I myself will search for my sheep, and will seek them out.
Ezekiel 34:11 (NRSV)

On my way to work, I drive past a sheep farm with lush pasture. One day I noticed a young lamb outside the fence near the road. Grazing on the newly found grass, it appeared unaware of potential danger from passing cars. Despite desperate calls from its mother on the other side of the fence, the lamb continued grazing.

I parked nearby to consider the best way to help the lamb. Depending upon my approach, it might head in the wrong direction, risking injury or worse. I ran to the nearby house and found a farm worker outside, and I was able to tell him about my discovery. After expressing his gratitude, he followed me back to the road and lifted the lamb over the fence. A sense of peace came over me as I watched the animal rejoin its mother.

Then I began to think about the times I have wandered away from God. For a short time, the new experience brought me happiness but, after realising my error, I asked for forgiveness and the strength to avoid making the same mistake again. When we focus on God's directions in the Bible, we are better able to walk along the right path. We can feel comfort and rest in knowing that when we stray, God guides us back to safety.

Prayer: *Dear God, thank you for your guidance and protection. Amen*

Thought for the day: Like a shepherd leads his sheep, God will lead me to shelter.

Nancy Frantel (Virginia, US)

God is great

Read Psalm 121:1–8

Look! The Lord does not lack the power to save, nor are his ears too dull to hear.
Isaiah 59:1 (CEB)

On 17 July 2015 doctors discovered that I had a 6.2 cm tumour, and I was diagnosed with pancreatic cancer. My wife, children and I decided to inform the minister of our church so that church members, along with our family and friends, could pray for me.

My treatment began with six rounds of chemotherapy. After those treatments, doctors performed another scan to check my progress. The results showed that the tumour had disappeared and that the cancer markers in my bloodstream were drastically reduced. I knew that God had performed a great miracle.

When I was first diagnosed, the doctor had informed my wife and brother that I might not live to see the year 2016. But by God's grace, I did. I am grateful for my doctors, six rounds of chemo and the miraculous power of our great God, who heard the prayers that everyone in my church said for me. In gratitude for this miracle of life, I have begun serving in my church as a committee member, and God is using my gifts and services. I am reminded that no matter what challenge we are facing, our God is great. He hears our prayers and will see us through.

Prayer: *O God, we give you glory, praise and honour for hearing our prayers and healing our diseases. Amen*

Thought for the day: In all situations I will put my faith in God.

Robinbhai P. Christian (Gujarat, India)

The pelican

Read Matthew 6:25–34

[Jesus said,] 'Don't worry about your life… Look at the birds in the sky. They don't sow seed or harvest grain or gather crops into barns. Yet your heavenly Father feeds them.'
Matthew 6:25–26 (CEB)

I love pelicans, not for their beauty but for their grace. Watching them glide through the sky calms my soul. Lately, my soul has needed calming. I have been diligently searching for work, but I have met rejection at every turn. Despite my constant pleading prayers, God has remained silent.

One day I was sitting on the beach praying as I watched the turquoise waves roll on to the shore. I saw a pelican soaring through the sky, and as I watched it searching the waves for fish, I pleaded with God again to show me what I should do with my life. As the bird soared above the water keeping watch for its next meal, it spotted a fish and immediately dived in to catch it. Then the pelican emerged from the water and floated atop the gentle waves as it enjoyed its dinner.

As I watched the pelican, my heart recognised God's message: 'Trust me. I am taking care of you.' It was a balm for my weary soul. As God provides for the pelican, so he provides for me.

Prayer: *Source of all that we have and are, help us to trust that you will provide for us and to be courageous enough to dive in when new opportunities come along. Amen*

Thought for the day: I will trust God to provide for me today.

Pamela Hutto (Florida, US)

Still climbing

Read Philippians 3:10–16

I press on towards the goal to win the prize for which God has called me heavenwards in Christ Jesus.
Philippians 3:14 (NIV)

What do you consider to be the mountaintop experiences of your Christian journey? For me, there have been many during more than 60 years as a Christian. They have come from many different sources: when the word of God has spoken very directly into my need; in times of worship with others or during my own quiet times; through reading Christian books; and through personal circumstances which drew me closer to the Lord. The most thrilling of all have been when I have been able to help and encourage someone else to grow in faith and commitment to the Lord.

We often have to overcome disappointments and setbacks along our way, demanding more trust and perseverance before victory over our circumstances can be won. Every time we stand on a peak we gain a clearer view of our ultimate destination and a greater determination to keep climbing.

As we read above, Paul always had his sights set on the ultimate goal, and was prepared to keep pressing on, straining towards the prize that lay ahead, even through such trials as shipwreck and imprisonment.

All who continue climbing to the end of this present life will see God face-to-face and spend eternity with him. What a prospect to spur us on to greater heights!

Prayer: *Lord, lead us onwards and upwards to our goal: life with you. Amen*

Thought for the day: I will treasure each day's opportunities.

Hazel Thompson (Somerset, England)

God cares

Read John 11:1–15

Jesus said, 'Did I not tell you that if you believe, you will see the glory of God?'
John 11:40 (NIV)

I had been crying out to God asking for a particular door to open for me, and when the door did not open I grew depressed and doubtful. I began to feel that God did not care about me.

I wonder if Mary and Martha felt the same way in today's reading. Mary, Martha and Lazarus were all friends of Jesus, and John 11 makes it clear that Jesus loved them. Yet when Lazarus was ill and they sent for Jesus, he didn't go immediately and Lazarus died. However, as soon as Jesus got the message that Lazarus was ill, he already had a plan for good, even though things seemed to be getting worse.

This passage of scripture reminds me that God also loves me, hears me when I call out, and is ready with an answer. God is able to fulfil the purpose for my life in his own time. All I am required to do is to keep believing.

Prayer: *Dear God, thank you for working all things to your glory. When life seems out of control, help us to trust you. We pray as Jesus taught us, saying, 'Our Father which art in heaven, Hallowed be thy name. Thy kingdom come. Thy will be done, as in heaven, so in earth. Give us day by day our daily bread. And forgive us our sins; for we also forgive every one that is indebted to us. And lead us not into temptation; but deliver us from evil.'* Amen*

Thought for the day: Even in the midst of pain, God is with me.

Tola Babalola (Lagos, Nigeria)

*Luke 11:2–4 (KJV)

A heart full of praise

Read Psalm 92:1–5

Be filled with the Spirit, speaking to one another with psalms, hymns, and songs from the Spirit. Sing and make music from your heart to the Lord.
Ephesians 5:18–19 (NIV)

I am not a trained or talented musician, but when I was young I always enjoyed singing in school choirs and singing praises to the Lord in church. A few years ago a viral infection attacked my vocal cords and left me with a condition called vocal cord paralysis. Because of this, I have difficulty speaking loudly or for long periods of time. My vocal cords become fatigued, and I may sound hoarse or have to take extra breaths. Singing, reading aloud to my grandchildren and public speaking have become challenging.

Initially it saddened and embarrassed me when, after singing a song or two during church services, I would have to stop completely. Not only was I giving up something I delighted in, but I was also giving up something that I know pleases God. However, lately I have decided simply to enjoy the music others are making. And I've discovered that when I am reading the words as I listen to them, I am better able to focus on the meaning of the hymns and songs.

I no longer feel robbed of the ability to praise the Lord with singing. Instead, I feel blessed to worship with new appreciation and understanding. My heart is full of praise.

Prayer: *O Lord, help us live in a way that pleases you. May our actions as well as our words be a song of praise to your most holy name. Amen*

Thought for the day: The Lord hears what is in my heart.

Jennifer B. Jones (New York, US)

Beautifully diverse

Read Romans 12:3–13

You are the body of Christ, and each one of you is a part of it.
1 Corinthians 12:27 (NIV)

For my birthday, my wife surprised me with a trip to a bird reserve. We saw birds from all over the world in many colours and sizes. Some were iridescent and bright, showing off an array of colours, while others wore earth tones of brown, green and grey. As I marvelled at the beautiful diversity of these creatures, I thought of another wonderful part of God's creation – humanity. We are also beautifully diverse – varying in culture, language and appearance.

We each have different experiences, gifts and stories to share. Even within our own communities, no two of us are exactly alike. Yet, like the birds, we are united by one creator – our loving God, who fashioned each of us uniquely with love and purpose.

This truth leads us to celebrate one another with respect, humility and compassion, for we are all made in the image of God. Our diversity is a wonderful display of God's creativity. Though different, each voice is important. We each have something to teach, and we all have much to learn. In a world so often divided, may we as Christ's followers model what it means to be diverse and yet united as we honour and cherish one another.

Prayer: *God of creation, thank you for the diversity in our world. Help us to be respectful and compassionate towards others as we celebrate your goodness and creativity. Amen*

Thought for the day: I will honour each person I encounter today as someone created in God's image.

Tyler Wood (North Carolina, US)

Running a good race

Read 2 Timothy 4:6–8

I have fought the good fight, I have finished the race, I have kept the faith.
2 Timothy 4:7 (NIV)

My husband, Kurt, and I used to walk a mile each day. Besides getting exercise, we enjoyed lively conversation and simply being together. But after Kurt passed away, I stopped taking walks. It simply wasn't enjoyable walking alone. However, when I finally convinced myself that I needed to exercise for my health, I started walking again.

As Christians, we are to run the race. While I know this verse from 2 Timothy isn't literally about running, it reminds me to push on with my life even though Kurt is gone. Walking alone gives me the opportunity to pray or quietly sing songs of praise to God.

Throughout his battle with cancer, Kurt fought the good fight. He finished his race, never wavering in his faith. Yes, I'm lonely. But with Christ's help, I can run the race, too. We are never truly alone when Jesus is running with us.

Prayer: *Lord God, thank you for sending Jesus to walk through life with us so that we are never truly alone. Help us to keep our faith strong until the very end. Amen*

Thought for the day: I may feel lonely, but in Christ I'm never alone.

Sue Carloni (Wisconsin, US)

Flourish again

Read John 15:1–8

[Jesus said,] 'I am the true vine, and my Father is the gardener. He cuts off every branch in me that bears no fruit, while every branch that does bear fruit he prunes so that it will be even more fruitful.'
John 15:1–2 (NIV)

Fire destroyed the retreat centre's main building, which housed the chapel, dining room and kitchen. One year later, I looked at the trees that had been in close proximity to the fire. Green leaves fluttered in stark contrast to scorched bark and dead, blackened branches. I could still see life in the trees, but I wondered whether they would survive. Experts advised cutting off all the dead branches to allow the trees to heal, grow and flourish once again.

The trees reminded me of today's reading. Even healthy trees need pruning – cutting away anything that prevents them from producing the best fruit. Jesus tells us that we are like branches that only survive if we remain in him, the true vine. We all make decisions and have attitudes – fear, disobedience, despair – that hinder us from attaining the fullness that God wants for us. But when we ask, God will prune away the old habits and replace them with life-giving ones.

Prayer: *Dear God, help us to remain in you so that we may have abundant life. Amen*

Thought for the day: What habits or attitudes will I ask God to prune from my life?

Carol Harrison (Saskatoon, Canada)

Small group questions

Wednesday 1 May

1 Describe a time when your small actions made a big difference for someone. How did this experience encourage you?

2 Who in your life, like Willy, simply needs to be heard? How will you make sure this person knows that you hear and love them?

3 Do you have loved ones who have suffered a stroke or some other debilitating health issue? In what ways do you show them Christ's love? In what ways do you encourage them?

4 Today's writer witnesses through his actions, rather than always talking about God. Is it always beneficial to witness primarily through actions or does it depend on the situation?

5 Willy said, 'That isn't for me. I am okay as I am.' Have there been times in your life when you've felt a similar way about God? What caused you to feel this way, and what brought you back to him?

Wednesday 8 May

1 Today's writer helped Aung Lin by bringing him food and money and by showing God's love to him. What does showing God's love to others look like to you?

2 What talents do you possess that you can use to help others and glorify God? If you have talents that you don't share with others, what is holding you back?

3 Does your church or your community have an organised effort to help refugees and others in need? If so, describe it. If not, what are some ways you could help on your own and encourage others to join you?

4 Is it difficult for you to find the time and energy to serve others? Like the author, do you wonder if you can make a difference in other people's lives? How do you combat these doubts and difficulties?

5 Recall a time when God led you to someone in need. How did you respond? How do you make sure that your heart and mind are open to those who need your help?

Wednesday 15 May

1 Have you or a loved one ever been given a frightening diagnosis? How did you overcome the fear you felt? What scripture passages comforted you during that time?

2 Describe an experience that reminded you that God was bigger than your problems. How does that experience encourage you now?

3 Recall a time when you relied on God to help you overcome fear. Did you experience relief from the weight of worry? What did that look like for you?

4 What can you do to encourage someone who is dealing with health issues? How can your church community show them love and help them through this challenging time?

5 When in your life have you had the choice to trust God or give in to fear? What did you choose? What scripture passages and spiritual practices helped you make your decision?

Wednesday 22 May

1 Describe a situation when you were not on the frontlines of God's work. Did you remain engaged in the situation or did you remove yourself from it? Why?

2 What does it look like to keep watch and remain engaged in the work of God? What spiritual practices help to keep you excited about God's work in the world?

3 What opportunities does your church offer that allow you to engage in the work of God? Do you participate on the frontlines? If so, describe your experience. If not, how do you support and engage with those opportunities from the sidelines?

4 Have you ever had a friend who was going through trials and needed you to keep watch with them, as Jesus asked of his disciples? How were you able to remain engaged and provide support and companionship for this person?

5 How do you know when you are being called to work or to cheer from the sidelines? Have there been times when you did not like what God was calling you to do? Describe those times and explain how you responded.

Wednesday 29 May

1 When you're experiencing a crisis, do you find it difficult to be still? Why? What can you do to encourage yourself to lean in and trust God during such times?

2 Recall a time when you did not remain calm during a crisis. Recall a time when you did. What affected your responses in each situation?

3 What scripture passages help you to find peace during times of struggle? Do you find comfort in fellowship with other believers during these times or do you prefer solitary worship? Why?

4 Have you ever felt as though God was not helping you out of a crisis in the way you would have liked? How did you keep trusting in God to resolve the situation, even if it was not the resolution you would have chosen?

5 What advice would you give to a friend or loved one who is struggling to remain still during a difficult time? How would you encourage them to find peace?

Wednesday 5 June

1 How do you outwardly express your faith? Do you find it difficult or easy to openly share your faith with others? Why?

2 Who in your life serves as a role model for you in their expression of faith, as Lainie does for the writer? Do you think it is important to have faith role models? Why or why not?

3 Have you experienced rejection or anger from others after sharing your faith with them? If not, why do you think you have only had positive experiences? If you have experienced anger or rejection, describe your experience. What was your reaction?

4 Have you ever felt embarrassed to share your faith with others? If so, how did you overcome your embarrassment?

5 How does your church community encourage you to participate in outward expressions of faith? In what ways do you share God with others in your church?

Wednesday 12 June

1 Today's writer describes her spiritual practice of memorising scripture verses. Do you memorise scripture as a part of your spiritual practice? If so, how does this help your faith journey? What other spiritual practices help you to strengthen your relationship with God?

2 When you're feeling lonely and homesick, how do you find peace and comfort? How does your faith help you through these times?

3 The writer enjoyed communing with God by the lake. Do you enjoy spending time with God in nature as well? If so, what do you appreciate most about it? If not, what is your preferred location for spending time with God and why?

4 Someone encouraged the writer by giving her a list of Bible verses to memorise while she was away from home. Who in your community is far from home at the moment? How can you encourage them and show them God's love?

5 When have you felt God's peace during a difficult time? How did feeling his peace change your experience?

Wednesday 19 June

1 Would you agree that we are living in a great era? Why or why not? How does your faith affect your answer?

2 What does it mean to live your faith during difficult times? How will you use the opportunities you have to proclaim the gospel to an uncertain world?

3 What do you think is the most effective way in which your church reaches out to the community? Why do you think it is the most effective way?

4 Which scripture passages encourage you when you feel over-whelmed by the negative events in the world? Why do they bring you such comfort?

5 Do you find it difficult to remain steadfast for Christ when you see pain in the world? How do you keep your faith strong despite trials and suffering? What advice would you give a loved one who is strug-gling to remain steadfast in their faith?

Wednesday 26 June

1 Describe a time when you experienced tension in a relationship and how you responded. Did you embrace a new attitude and change the situation, or not? How does your mindset affect your interactions with others?

2 In what ways do you honour those around you? How have you been honoured by others? What does it mean to you to 'outdo one another in showing honour'?

3 With whom in your life have you had a difficult relationship lately? How can you turn that situation into one of love and respect?

4 How do you avoid keeping score with those around you? What prac-tices help you to love and honour those who offend you or wrong you?

5 When members of your church or community have disagreements, how do they resolve them? What does this teach you about how you would like to respond to conflict in your life?

Wednesday 3 July

1 When have you decided to take a risk that others did not understand or tried to discourage you from taking? Did their concerns make you think differently about your decision? Did you take the risk after all?

2 Can you relate to the writer's experience of feeling called by God to a particular place or kind of work? How do you listen for God's guidance? What practices help you to determine God's will for your life?

3 When you encounter opposition or disagreement from others about your beliefs or actions, how do you respond? What have you learned from these experiences?

4 Do you think others can see your faith in the actions and decisions you make? If so, how? If not, how can you help others to see that your faith informs your daily decisions?

5 Today's writer says that we sometimes need to take risks to make ourselves available to God. When has this been true in your experience?

Wednesday 10 July

1 If you know someone like Thad's mother, for whom it is natural and easy to talk to strangers about faith, what do you admire about that person? Is this kind of witness easy or difficult for you? Why?

2 To whom do you look as a model for sharing your faith? Give some examples of how this person has shared his or her faith with you and why it was meaningful or memorable to you.

3 Do you believe there is a right way to share your faith with others? If so, describe it and explain why this way is best. If not, explain why.

4 Name some ways in which people share their faith in the Bible. Which of these people do you relate to most? Which person do you want to be more like? Explain.

5 How does your church share its faith with your community? How could it be better at sharing faith? What examples would you offer to other churches as good ways to witness to people outside the church walls?

Wednesday 17 July

1   As a child, did you go to church and participate in church activities? What role did faith play in your family life? In what ways has your faith changed over time? In what ways has it remained the same?

2   How do you respond when you hear about someone's life-changing encounter with God? Can you relate to these kinds of stories? Is it difficult for you to understand?

3   When you experience a crisis, how do you pray? What do you pray for? How have your prayers been answered?

4   What helps you to feel assured of God's power and presence in your life? Describe the practices, prayers, Bible readings or people that help you feel connected to God.

5   How does your church community pray for one another? How do people request prayer? Have you experienced the prayers of others to be meaningful in your times of struggle? How could your church pray more regularly for one another and for people around the world?

Wednesday 24 July

1   How do you identify yourself? By your job? Your relationships? How you spend your free time? What would make you feel as if you had lost your identity?

2   When have you taken a job or offered to help with a task that you were unenthusiastic about? Did your perspective about the work change after you completed the task? Explain.

3   In what setting would you be most surprised to find yourself ministering to others? Why would it surprise you?

4   Recall a time when a conversation with someone you had just met made a lasting impression on you. Describe the conversation. What was it about that conversation that was meaningful to you?

5   Name some Bible stories where someone begins a new life or ministry. Which of these do you most identify with? What do the stories you named have in common with each other and with today's meditation?

Wednesday 31 July

1   Have you ever read the Bible from beginning to end? If so, describe your experience. If not, why?

2   How often do you read the Bible? What tools and resources help you to connect with God through scripture?

3   How does your church use the Bible in worship and teaching? What other times or ways would you like to see your church community engage with scripture?

4   When you read the Bible, which books, verses or stories are most meaningful to you? Which parts of the Bible are difficult for you to read? Which parts of scripture are you least familiar with?

5   Name a Bible passage that has held a different message or importance for you at different times in your life. Why do you think this is the case? What has this taught you about God's word?

Wednesday 7 August

1   Have you ever made a garden or cultivated plants? If so, what was your favourite part of that work? What was challenging about it? What did you learn from tending plants?

2   In what areas of your life have you seen God's transforming work? In what areas of your life do you hope for God's transforming work?

3   Today's writer can see the future of a pea plant from a tiny seed. What examples from nature or your own life help you to see or have hope for the future?

4   What does the resurrection mean to you? How does your faith in Christ's redeeming love shape the way you think and act?

5 How does your church help people to understand and embrace the transformation that is possible through faith in Christ? In what ways could you imagine this important message being shared more clearly and more widely?

Wednesday 14 August

1 When were you most recently disappointed? What disappointed you? How did you deal with your feelings?

2 Have you ever encountered someone in an unexpected place and then become friends with that person? What do you remember about your first conversation with this person?

3 How did you first encounter God? Who or what helped you to experience his presence for the first time? How did this encounter shape the way you understand him?

4 What small miracle or insight from God have you witnessed or received recently? Describe the circumstances. How did the miracle or insight affect how you felt about the situation?

5 How does your church encourage people experiencing difficulties? How does your church help people to know God in new ways and to trust him more fully?

Wednesday 21 August

1 If you have ever witnessed the solar eclipse, describe your experience. If you have not, describe an experience when you observed a diverse group of people moving beyond their differences towards unity.

2 How do you remain focused on God? When you realise that you have lost your focus on him, what practices or people help you to regain focus?

3 In what ways does your church community encourage you to look beyond the differences you have with others? In what ways do you think your church community could become more unified?

4 Describe a time when you felt wonder at God's creation. Did your experience change the way you feel about the world and those around you? Why or why not?

5 Which scripture passages remind you of the greatness of God's creation? What scripture passages encourage you to reflect God's love to others, regardless of your differences?

Wednesday 28 August

1 The writer finds a new appreciation for the words of hymns when she does not sing. Have you ever listened to others singing in worship instead of joining in? How is your worship experience different when you simply listen to the hymns?

2 Do you ever feel embarrassed or self-conscious during worship? What makes you feel that way? What might help you avoid feeling embarrassed during worship?

3 Is singing a significant part of worship in your church? What other aspects of worship are prominent in your church services? What do you wish your church would emphasise more during worship? Why?

4 Describe a time when you were unable to worship in the way you prefer. What did you learn about yourself or about worship from that experience? What other forms of worship could you practise during those times?

5 How can you make your actions and words be a song of praise to God? What does it look like to live your life praising him?

Journal page

Journal page

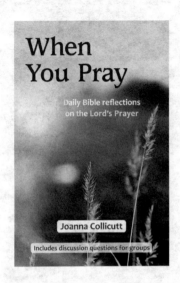

In this updated edition of a classic text, Joanna Collicutt shows how growing as a Christian is rooted in the prayer Jesus gave us. As we pray the Lord's Prayer, we express our relationship with God, absorb gospel values and are also motivated to live them out. As we pray to the Father, in union with the Son, through the power of the Spirit, we begin to take on the character of Christ.

When You Pray
Daily Bible reflections on the Lord's Prayer
Joanna Collicutt
978 0 85746 867 3 £9.99
brfonline.org.uk

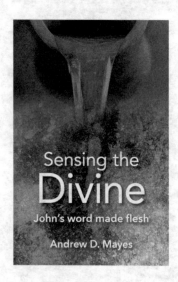

This compelling, inspiring book is an invigorating rereading of the fourth gospel by a well-known spirituality writer who has lived some years in the Holy Land. Uniquely, it approaches John's gospel by exploring how he uses the senses, both physical and spiritual, in his encounter with Jesus Christ, the Word made flesh. This refreshing appreciation of the gospel will activate and stimulate our own discoveries and spiritual quest, not only of the gospel, but also of God's world, ourselves and our mission.

Sensing the Divine
John's word made flesh
Andrew D. Mayes
978 0 85746 658 7 £9.99
brfonline.org.uk

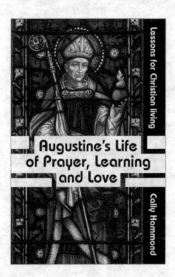

The book tells the story of Augustine as an example to inspire and encourage today's Christian. It takes the reader from Augustine's first beginnings of faith, struggles with doubt, fear of scorn and mockery, worries about whether he is 'good enough', through public affirmation and church membership, into the dedicated life of worship, Bible reading, thinking about faith and living it. It concludes with moments of prayer from Augustine's life, encouraging the reader to take the next steps in thought and prayer that God is calling them to.

Augustine's Life of Prayer, Learning and Love
Lessons for Christian living
Cally Hammond
978 0 85746 713 3 £9.99
brfonline.org.uk

Books on prayer can so often make us feel challenged but guilty. Not this one! *Prayer in the Making* is a book for everyone wanting to pray more confidently. Because we are all different, we need to find the prayer life that fits with who God made us to be. Lyndall Bywater explores twelve different types of prayer, helping us to find the ones which best suit us and our lifestyles. She certainly challenges us, but leaves us ready to talk confidently with God.

Prayer in the Making
Trying it, talking it, sustaining it
Lyndall Bywater
978 0 85746 801 7 £8.99
brfonline.org.uk

How to encourage Bible reading in your church

BRF has been helping individuals connect with the Bible for over 90 years. We want to support churches as they seek to encourage church members into regular Bible reading.

Order a Bible reading resources pack
This pack is designed to give your church the tools to publicise our Bible reading notes. It includes:

- Sample Bible reading notes for your congregation to try.
- Publicity resources, including a poster.
- A church magazine feature about Bible reading notes.

The pack is free, but we welcome a £5 donation to cover the cost of postage. If you require a pack to be sent outside the UK or require a specific number of sample Bible reading notes, please contact us for postage costs. More information about what the current pack contains is available on our website.

How to order and find out more
- Visit **biblereadingnotes.org.uk/for-churches**.
- Telephone BRF on +44 (0)1865 319700 Mon–Fri 9.15–17.30.
- Write to us at BRF, 15 The Chambers, Vineyard, Abingdon OX14 3FE.

Keep informed about our latest initiatives
We are continuing to develop resources to help churches encourage people into regular Bible reading, wherever they are on their journey. Join our email list at **brfonline.org.uk/signup** to stay informed about the latest initiatives that your church could benefit from.

Subscriptions

The Upper Room is published in January, May and September.

Individual subscriptions
The subscription rate for orders for 4 or fewer copies includes postage and packing:

The Upper Room annual individual subscription £17.40

Group subscriptions
Orders for 5 copies or more, sent to ONE address, are post free:
The Upper Room annual group subscription £13.80

Please do not send payment with order for a group subscription. We will send an invoice with your first order.

Please note that the annual billing period for group subscriptions runs from 1 May to 30 April.

Copies of the notes may also be obtained from Christian bookshops.

Single copies of *The Upper Room* cost £4.60.

Prices valid until 30 April 2020.

Giant print version
The Upper Room is available in giant print for the visually impaired, from:

Torch Trust for the Blind
Torch House
Torch Way
Northampton Road
Market Harborough   Tel: +44 (0)1858 438260
LE16 9HL   **torchtrust.org**

THE UPPER ROOM: INDIVIDUAL/GIFT SUBSCRIPTION FORM

> **All our Bible reading notes can be ordered online by visiting biblereadingnotes.org.uk/subscriptions**

☐ I would like to take out a subscription myself (complete your name and address details once)

☐ I would like to give a gift subscription (please provide both names and addresses)

Title .... First name/initials .... Surname ....

Address ....

.... Postcode ....

Telephone .... Email ....

Gift subscription name ....

Gift subscription address ....

.... Postcode ....

Gift message (20 words max. or include your own gift card):

....

....

Please send *The Upper Room* beginning with the September 2019 / January 2020 / May 2020 issue (*delete as appropriate*):

Annual individual subscription ☐ £17.40   Total enclosed £ ....

Method of payment

☐ Cheque (made payable to BRF) ☐ MasterCard / Visa

Card no. ☐☐☐☐ ☐☐☐☐ ☐☐☐☐ ☐☐☐☐

Expires end ☐ M ☐ M ☐ Y ☐ Y   Security code* ☐☐☐ Last 3 digits on the reverse of the card

*ESSENTIAL IN ORDER TO PROCESS THE PAYMENT

> **All our Bible reading notes can be ordered online by visiting
> biblereadingnotes.org.uk/subscriptions**

❏ Please send me .... copies of *The Upper Room* September 2019 /
January 2020 / May 2020 issue (*delete as appropriate*)

Title .... First name/initials .... Surname ....

Address ....

.... Postcode ....

Telephone .... Email ....

Please do not send payment with this order. We will send an invoice with
your first order.

Christian bookshops: All good Christian bookshops stock BRF publications.
For your nearest stockist, please contact BRF.

Telephone: The BRF office is open Mon–Fri 9.15–17.30. To place your order,
telephone +44 (0)1865 319700.

Online: biblereadingnotes.org.uk/group-subscriptions

❏ Please send me a Bible reading resources pack to encourage Bible
reading in my church

Please return this form with the appropriate payment to:
BRF, 15 The Chambers, Vineyard, Abingdon OX14 3FE
To read our terms and find out about cancelling your order, please visit **brfonline.org.uk/terms**.

BRF

To order

Online: **brfonline.org.uk**
Telephone: +44 (0)1865 319700 Mon–Fri 9.15–17.30

Delivery times within the UK are normally 15 working days. Prices are correct at the time of going to press but may change without prior notice.

Title	Price	Qty	Total
When You Pray	£9.99		
Sensing the Divine	£9.99		
Augustine's Life of Prayer, Learning and Love	£9.99		
Prayer in the Making	£8.99		

POSTAGE AND PACKING CHARGES			
Order value	UK	Europe	Rest of world
Under £7.00	£2.00	£5.00	£7.00
£7.00–£29.99	£3.00	£9.00	£15.00
£30.00 and over	FREE	£9.00 + 15% of order value	£15.00 + 20% of order value

Total value of books	
Postage and packing	
Donation	
Total for this order	

Please complete in BLOCK CAPITALS

Title .... First name/initials .... Surname...................................

Address...

.... Postcode ....

Acc. No. .... Telephone ....

Email..

Method of payment

☐ Cheque (made payable to BRF) ☐ MasterCard / Visa

Card no. ⬚⬚⬚⬚ ⬚⬚⬚⬚ ⬚⬚⬚⬚ ⬚⬚⬚⬚ ⬚⬚⬚⬚

Expires end ⬚⬚ ⬚⬚ Security code* ⬚⬚⬚ Last 3 digits on the reverse of the card

Signature* .... Date ..../........../..........

*ESSENTIAL IN ORDER TO PROCESS YOUR ORDER

The Bible Reading Fellowship Gift Aid Declaration

giftaid it

Please treat as Gift Aid donations all qualifying gifts of money made

☐ today, ☐ in the past four years, ☐ and in the future **or** ☐ My donation does not qualify for Gift Aid.

I am a UK taxpayer and understand that if I pay less Income Tax and/or Capital Gains Tax in the current tax year than the amount of Gift Aid claimed on all my donations, it is my responsibility to pay any difference.

Please notify BRF if you want to cancel this declaration, change your name or home address, or no longer pay sufficient tax on your income and/or capital gains.

Please return this form to: BRF, 15 The Chambers, Vineyard, Abingdon OX14 3FE | **enquiries@brf.org.uk**
To read our terms and find out about cancelling your order, please visit **brfonline.org.uk/terms**.

The Bible Reading Fellowship (BRF) is a Registered Charity (233280)

IR0219